VW CAMPER
BUYERS' GUIDE

A catalogue record for this book is available from the British Library

ISBN 978-0-9928769-1-3

Published by Behemoth Publishing

59 High Street, Wincanton, Somerset BA9 9JZ, UK

www.behemothpublishing.co.uk

Printed and bound in the UK by Cambrian Printers

Edited by Derek Smith

Designed by Richard Parsons

Cover pictures © Richard Copping except front cover, lower image:
© Magic Car Pics (www.magiccarpics.co.uk)

Archive material sourced from the library collated by Richard Copping
All imagery copyright respective camper conversion companies apart from
Volkswagen Alktiengesellschaft/Volkswagen of America

Pages 6/7, 8, 9, 10, 11, 15 (top and bottom), 16/17, 19, 20, 22, 23, 24, 25, 29, 32, 34, 35, 37, 38, 39, 40/41, 45, 98 (top), 104, 105, 112, 114, 115, 116, 117, 118, 119, 126, 129, 131, 133, 143, 152, 153, 154, 156, 157, 208, 209, 210, 211, 212.

VW CAMPER
BUYERS' GUIDE

BEHEMOTH
PUBLISHING
www.behemothpublishing.co.uk

CONTENTS

	INTRODUCTION	6
CHAPTER 1	BACK TO SCHOOL FOR A VW HISTORY LESSON	10
CHAPTER 2	PRIMARY USAGE – MARKS OUT OF TEN	42
CHAPTER 3	CONCERNING MATTERS BUDGETARY	60
CHAPTER 4	CLASSIC CONVERSIONS OUTLINED	112
CHAPTER 5	CUSTOMISING YOUR CAMPER	158
CHAPTER 6	PIECES OF PAPER, THE TIN WORM AND OILY BITS	184
CHAPTER 7	IN WHICH YOU ARE TOLD WHERE TO GO	220

INTRODUCTION

By purchasing this book, half the battle is already won. The talk, the tale, the advice is exclusively Volkswagen related – in the view of most owners past and present, the best of the breed. VW Campers, dependent on the model, are about a combination of ageless design, enduring quality, unparalleled longevity, reliability, value for money and even investment potential.

Buy the right one and endless pleasure awaits you: away-from-it-all camping weekends and hotel-free holidays full of adventure, rousing enthusiast gatherings at home and abroad, wonderfully friendly clubs and knowledgeable communities, a world of bespoke interiors, enthralling restorations, amazing concours triumphs and, ultimately, whatever emerges as your particular delight. The purpose of this book is to guide you towards making the right decision for you.

That's the good news, but horrors might also lurk in the shadows.

Rust in abundance, restorations full of filler, near unsaleable wrecks, purchases made at vastly inflated prices, or simply the pleasure-spoiling wrong model for you. This book will help you avoid the ambushes that can beset those who rush in where even fools fear to tread.

The choice open to you is enormous, after all the VW Transporter (on which the Camper is based) has been in production since 1950. You could buy an in-vogue veteran, split screen and all, built before the summer of 1967. That's the one featured on all the gift-shop trinkets, an idyllic, even iconic, classic. Also beloved of the nation is its successor, the panoramic windscreen, retro-appealing 'Bay', a product of the late sixties and the 1970s. It probably won't cost you as much as a 'Split' and is undoubtedly more practical (if both heavy on fuel and sluggish in some guises). There's even the option of a Brazilian-built lookalike, which stayed in production until the end of 2013! Less expensive by far and full of 1980s creature comforts and gadgetry is Volkswagen's third-generation Camper, a vehicle that started life using the company's traditional air-cooled technology but later embraced its own unique take on water-cooling and the first diesel engine to propel a Transporter.

⬇ Plenty to choose from! When this photograph was taken by Volkswagen, there were four generations of VW Camper. In 2015 there are six ... a VW for everyone.

MH⋅EC 980   WOB⋅JC 204

Three generations of VW California with, from left to right, the facelift T5 (2010–2015), Westfalia's T3 (1988–1990) and the long-nose version of the T4 (1996–2003).

From 1990 until 2003 there was the distinctly stylish T4, to all intents and purposes still a modern, high-specification Camper, a belle which embraced both genuinely powerful petrol engines and economical yet pace-setting diesels. In the footsteps of the first front-wheel-drive, front-engine Transporter came the T5, the elegant and sophisticated fifth-generation model and the first to be offered as a Camper built by Volkswagen, rather than converted by approved coachworks and companies on their behalf. September 2009 saw an updated T5 launched and the advent of models with new, even more powerful, but also more economical, leaner and greener engines.

All five generations are out there to purchase and readily available although in many cases at a price. Specialist dealers and in some instances importers, website sales, conversion companies, private individuals and Volkswagen Van Centres all offer potential owners scope to find the Camper they are looking for. Indeed, the Van Centre will inevitably be able to supply a brand new VW Camper if that is the ultimate choice; just as a string of respected conversion companies will similarly offer their own take on the latest model. Each option will be right for someone and just as wrong for someone else.

The task in hand is to help determine the particular appeal of a given generation of VW Camper to you. What is high on your list of priorities? What should the vehicle be able to do? Is it to be a daily driver? Is originality paramount? Are appearances all consuming? Where do creature comforts rank? Is power, or the lack of it, significant? Is your budget unlimited? Do the joys of restoration outweigh all other considerations?

Each chapter, every page and paragraph, will bring you closer to your decision, but please note that when it comes to prices, here is a snapshot of a seasonally fluctuating market as it was at the launch of the T6.

Buying a VW Camper is a serious business, but it can, and should be, enormous fun too. Hopefully, you will find this book informative and enjoyable to browse or read line by line. Assuming some readers will dip in and out of the book, there has been a deliberate move to repeat salient points wherever they are particularly relevant. My apologies to the line-by-line reader...

⬇ Volkswagen's colour palette has invariably embodied good taste and the two shades of metallic blue, Olympia and Night, which formed part of the offer in the final year of T5 production are no exception.

CHAPTER 1
BACK TO SCHOOL FOR
A VW HISTORY LESSON

A s hinted in the introduction, the VW Camper is a derivative of the VW Transporter, Volkswagen's multi-use commercial/passenger carrying vehicle, a series of models launched to an assembly of expectant motoring journalists in late 1949. The full range, planned from the start, but developed and built at the VW factory over the next few years, did not include a Camper, but the Transporter's potential as such a vehicle was recognised by enterprising coachbuilders and craftsmen. Of the range built by Volkswagen, the most appropriate for conversion were the Micro Bus (a reasonably well appointed people carrier), Kombi (a Delivery Van with windows and easily removable 'load compartment' seating) or Delivery Van (the least popular of the three, as

⬇ Prototype VW Transporter Delivery Van as illustrated in the 1950 brochure 'VW-Lieferwagen Eine Bildserie'.

the conversion company had to add side windows). By the end of the 1950s, a considerable number of conversions were available in an ever-growing number of countries.

In Germany, what for Volkswagen and coachbuilder Westfalia had started as little more than an understated acknowledgement of each other's presence became formalised to such an extent that the converted vehicles exported to America were marketed as 'VW Campers with Westfalia De Luxe equipment'. Inevitably, Westfalia conversions could similarly be bought through home-market and other European dealerships. From that cementing of the relationship at the end of 1950s, the undoubtedly unequal partnership between Volkswagen and Westfalia remained intact until 2003 when, following the coachbuilder's acquisition by VW's rivals, the DaimlerChrysler group (now simply Daimler), Volkswagen developed its own conversion, the California, a Camper based on the fifth-generation Transporter.

It shouldn't be assumed that Westfalia was the only player in either Germany or the USA, merely the pioneer. Other manufacturers such

↑ The Micro Bus (and the less expensive VW Kombi) was an ideal vehicle to convert to a Camper. This is a 1949 prototype from the 1950 brochure 'VW-Lieferwagen Eine Bilderserie'.

DEFINITION OF A VW CAMPER

The VW Camper is a Volkswagen Transporter converted by an independent company approved or otherwise by the car manufacturer. From 2003, Volkswagen has produced its own Camper.

A NOTE ABOUT MODEL YEARS

Many sellers of older models will refer to their Camper as, for example, a 1960 model, when in reality it was built during 1959 and quite possibly first licensed for road use in that year. This is because with effect from August 1955, Volkswagen adopted the relatively common practice of introducing the next calendar year model after the factory summer holidays. Whereas previously when major specification changes were made, they might occur at any time in the year, from this point they tended to take place at the start of the new model year, although there are sufficient exceptions to the rule to destroy its infallibility.

The rules changed again at the end of the last century. The 1999 model year ended in April of that year so that Volkswagen cars and vans produced in May were marketed as 2000 model year vehicles. Model years still run from the beginning of May to the end of April (e.g. May 2014 to April 2015 is the 2015 model year).

as boat builders Dehler, the redoubtable Karmann coachworks and demountable specialists Tischer, all native to Germany, were active for at least part of the story. Dehler's conversions on the T3 were notably luxurious, Karmann (of Beetle Cabriolet and Karmann Ghia fame) specialised from the days of the second-generation Transporter in coach-built campers with an aluminium frame and insulated panels, while Tischer developed a demountable 'camper' to attach on the back of a VW Pick-up.

⬇ 'Westfalia presents the holiday home on wheels' – cover image from Westfalia's 1956 promotional offering.

In Britain, Camper conversion pioneers included Peter Pitt, Moortown Motors and, above all, Devon. The links to Volkswagen in Germany were more tenuous (Moortown were VW Distributors, while Devon models were sold through UK dealerships). In the 1960s, first Moortown and later Canterbury Pitt disappeared from the market while key players such as Dormobile and Danbury emerged. The former vanished at the end of the 1970s, while Danbury remained an important participant in the VW Camper game for much of the 1980s. After more than one change of ownership, Devon eventually turned its attention to brands other than Volkswagen as the 1990s dawned. Other companies took centre stage for a while, including Holdsworth, Viking (the trading name of Motorhomes International), and Autohomes, each succumbing to bankruptcy as the market became more difficult. One survivor from that era, Auto-Sleepers, now restricts its VW model output, but a plethora of smaller companies flood the market.

⬆ A glimpse of the luxurious Dehler Profi Camper based on the third-generation Transporter (from a mid-1980s brochure).

A NOTE REGARDING PFERDESTÄRKE (PS)

Volkswagen's home-market literature inevitably expressed performance in terms of metric horsepower, or *Pferdestärke* (PS). As British and US brake horsepower differ and the rules relating to the latter altered during the period covered by this book, for consistency PS has been used throughout.

To convert PS figures to British horsepower, multiply by 0.986.

1950–1967
THE FIRST-GENERATION VW CAMPER

There are many, many first-generation VW Campers on the highways and byways and, providing you are prepared to pay the price, you could be the proud owner of one remarkably quickly. However, the chances of finding a pre-March 1955 model in original condition are remote. Realistically only the dedicated vintage enthusiast would want to use one for anything other than occasional concours appearances anyway.

➜ Almost camping! This is a 1952 Micro Bus and the photograph clearly illustrates the pre-1955 'barn-door' engine lid. From the 1952 brochure, 'Volkswagen présente sa production au salon de Paris'.

➜ This cover image from Volkswagen's 1959 Camper brochure illustrates the bullet-shape indicators and the US-style two-tier bumpers.

The pre-March 1955 Transporter sports a remarkably large engine compartment lid and as a result is known by enthusiasts as the 'barn-door' model. The earliest models feature a crash gearbox and the 'original' 25PS Beetle engine. Performance is pedestrian to say the least – quoting either a top speed or the time taken to achieve 0–60mph is academic. A single binnacle is as close to a dashboard as you will get (on all but the Micro Bus De Luxe), while ventilation is grossly inadequate, leading to steamy windows at the slightest provocation.

The Transporter underwent a facelift in March 1955. The engine compartment and its lid became much smaller, making invaluable rearward access possible through an upward-lifting hatch. Ventilation was much improved, thanks to an air intake system above the vehicle's windscreen (noticeable in the redesigned roof panel with a peaked front). The dashboard was now full-length on all models. The engine was a 30PS unit and, although reliable, remained leisurely in performance terms compared to later engines. Electrics remained of

THE FIRST-GENERATION VW CAMPER

Length: 4,280mm
Width: 1,750mm
Height: 1,940mm

(1961 Micro Bus – dimensions vary slightly over the years and according to model. Note: Campers fitted with an elevating roof will carry a greater height even with the roof down.)

'Unitised, stiff all-steel box body' (taken from early VW literature), or, more accurately, body integral with the chassis. Structural rigidity achieved by two substantial longitudinal rails and five hefty cross-members and attendant outriggers. Independent torsion-bar suspension, hydraulic brakes. Initially, 1,131cc, 25PS at 3,300rpm, air-cooled engine at rear.

↑ From a brochure published in May 1965, this showroom image illustrates both the larger 'fish-eye' indicators at the front and the bigger window/hatch at the rear.

a 6-volt nature (and would do so until August 1966 and the last year of first-generation production). Barely visible semaphore indicators lingered as standard on European production models until the summer of 1960. However, vehicles destined for the United States acquired 'modern' bullet-shaped indicators at the front in 1955. VW Campers of mid to late 1950s vintage still in existence are rare machines.

The majority of surviving first-generation Campers date from the 1960s and in terms of practicality such models are a definite improvement on earlier versions. In June 1960 the vehicle's engine was upgraded to a 1,192cc, 34PS unit. A minority regard the introduction of an automatic choke at the same time as more of a hindrance than an asset. Of more significance to a vehicle the size and weight of a VW Camper was the arrival of a 1,493cc, 42PS engine at the start of 1963 (initially USA option only; from March, European spec too) and the final withdrawal of the 1200 in October 1965. July 1961 saw the arrival of modern segmented rear light clusters; the top section (red in the USA and orange in Europe) reflected an indicator bulb that flashed in unison with its partner at the front of the vehicle. Larger front indicators

(nicknamed fisheye flashers) debuted in the United States in July 1961 to be followed on European models in August 1963. Rearward visibility was enhanced and easier access afforded when a larger tailgate was introduced at the start of the 1964 model year in August 1963. A reduction in wheel size to 14in in December 1963 and more powerful self-parking wipers in August 1964 suggest the later the build date of a first-generation Transporter the more suitable it might be for regular (summer) use on today's roads. In the same manner, and finally, for the last year of production, 12-volt electrics became standard, although a lucky few might find the original owner had specified them as an extra-cost option (M620) in earlier years.

Although German first-generation Transporter production ended in July 1967, Brazilian manufacture of a similar vehicle continued until 1975. A small percentage of such vehicles were assembled in South Africa's Uitenhage factory, where they were sold alongside the new second-generation Transporter but at budget prices. The Kombi version of the Fleetline range, as these models were known, can occasionally be seen in Britain. None started life as Campers.

1967–1979
THE SECOND-GENERATION VW CAMPER

Escalating fuel costs, born out of the oil crises related to war and strife in the Middle East and in turn linked to prolonged and damaging recession in both Europe and the USA, affected both Transporter and Camper conversion numbers in the mid-1970s. Nevertheless, in its 12-year production run some 2,465,000 second-generation Transporters were built. This exceeded the 1,833,000 examples of its predecessor, which took 17½ years to amass. Similarly, this overwhelming figure exceeded those of following generations and it appears probable that the model produced in Germany between August 1967 and the end of July 1979 will retain record status in perpetuity. The VW Camper conversion companies, both new and well established, enjoyed a boom period in the last years of the 1960s and the first years of the new decade. As if to prove their good fortune, a deluge of new models appeared annually, and a good proportion of the best ones have survived in plentiful numbers.

Although later generations might have greater acreage of glass, the panoramic nature of the second-generation Transporter's windscreen (and much larger side windows) not only earned it the nickname of

THE SECOND-GENERATION VW CAMPER

Length: 4,420 mm
Width: 1,755mm
Height: 1,940 mm

(1969 Micro Bus, dimensions vary slightly over the years and according to model. Note: VW Campers with an elevating roof will stand higher, even with the roof down.)

Although demonstrating many similarities to its predecessor, the second-generation Transporter benefitted from a double-walled construction, which allowed the removal of the braces between the side windows characteristic of the earlier model. Reduction gearing and a swing axle were features relegated to the past, the latter being replaced by a double-jointed rear axle.

A new 47PS 1600 engine offered a 3PS increase over the outgoing 1500 of the first-generation Transporter, and further increases in engine size would become a hallmark of the second-generation Transporter's progress.

← The cover image of the 1970 brochure 'Der VW-Personentransporter' illustrates to perfection the characteristics of the early second-generation Transporter: panoramic screen, large VW roundel, indicators low down close to the rounded bumpers and external, rubber-covered cab steps.

the 'Bay' but also gave it a much more modern look than the 'Splitty'. (Despite its appearance, the windscreen was only 27 per cent larger than the combined panes of its predecessor.) Indeed, such was the happy, smiling nature of this fresh-faced design of the mid-1960s that, even decades later, the second-generation model still doesn't look dated but also offers a certain retro appeal.

As with the first-generation model, there is a distinct pre- and post-makeover look, the main changes occurring in August 1972 (for the '73 model year). While in official circles, and on the German enthusiast scene, the two variations are often referred to as the Type 2a and Type 2b respectively, in Britain and elsewhere the somewhat unimaginative devotee talk is of 'early' and 'late' second-generation (or early and late Bay) models.

The 'early' second-generation Transporter is easily identifiable by the large size of the VW roundel between its headlights, rectangular front indicators low down on its front panel and close to its rounded blade-style bumpers (which are similar to those of its predecessor).

↑ A side profile of the early second-generation Transporter in Westfalia Camper guise reproduced from a 1970 Dutch-market brochure.

External cabs steps, which appeared as an extension to the front bumper, were already antiquated when they were introduced in 1967 but now contribute to the vehicle's quirky retro appeal. The rear light clusters were initially almost identical to those of late first-generation Transporters although, as part of Hanover's makeover exercise, vehicles produced after August 1971 carried more substantial units. Until August 1970, second-generation Transporters featured the delightful painted or chromed domed hubcaps of earlier decades.

All Bays lack the disfiguring external hinges of the first-generation model, while the standard sliding side door (an extra-cost option on the first-generation from April 1963 but rarely included in the specification of a Camper conversion) is more in keeping with the look of vehicles produced today. As ventilation (in the form of a grille below the windscreen) was accommodated in the design of the front panel, the previous complicated arrangement of a peaked roof panel was no longer required. Modern wind-down cab windows replaced the elderly budget-style sliders, while the new dashboard, although spartan compared to the aeroplane cockpit-style ones of today, was partially trimmed with protective and reflection-free padded plastic. Flat rubber-edged protective control knobs (introduced in the final years of first-generation production) were retained, standing as a symbol of forthcoming measures to advance the safety aspects of Volkswagen's commercial or passenger-carrying vehicle.

The first tranche of such improvements came in August 1969 (for the '70 model year) when, although visually unchanged, the Transporter's doors were fitted with stronger frames to reduce the risk of injury in the event of impact from the side. Similarly, diagonal beams were added under the cab floor, offering more strength in the case of a collision.

Two changes made in the summer of 1970 (for the 1971 model year) are worthy of careful consideration. The first, and of greatest significance, was an engine upgrade.

The 1600 engine's cylinder heads were modified and featured twin inlet ports rather than single ones. As a result, the engine could breathe more easily and power duly increased from 47PS to a maximum of 50PS. Considering there are those that consider the twin-port engine to be a less reliable unit than its predecessor, perhaps the change could have been overlooked if it hadn't apparently set a precedent. As will be seen, larger and more powerful engines were introduced on a frequent basis for much of the second-generation Transporter's remaining years in production. While the 1600 twin-port remained an option (at least in Europe) and quite a number of Campers are so endowed, there will be ample opportunities for today's purchaser to find a vehicle with a better top speed and, perhaps more importantly, improved torque. Also, while there might be a slight penalty in terms of fuel consumption with the larger engine (for example, Volkswagen quoted 24.8mpg for the 1600 at the start of the '73 model year and 22.0mpg for the bigger engine of the day) neither are earth-shatteringly economical. Hence, many would choose to enjoy the benefit of additional power (maximum speed quoted for 1973 models as 68mph for the 1600 and 78mph for the larger engine).

To coincide with the arrival of the twin-port 1600, Volkswagen replaced the front brake drums with 278mm ATE discs, no doubt more to the reassurance of would-be Camper owners today than in the summer of 1970. Sadly, the attendant change of wheel design, which displaced the traditional four elongated ventilation slots between the rim and the centre, introduced a series of round holes punched through the steel. The design of the hubcaps was also revised, and the Transporter lost the attractive domed affairs that had been a feature since 1949 and joined other members of the VW family in offering flat hubcaps. Of more practical benefit to owners was the upgrading of the Transporter's relatively skinny 5J x 14 tyres to meatier 5½J x 14 rubber.

The 1972 model year saw the arrival of the 1700 engine as an additional more powerful option for those with reservations about the Transporter's performance. Unlike the upgraded 1600 of the previous year, this engine was borrowed from another Volkswagen, the largest of the air-cooled cars, the VW 411. As it had been designed to sit below a

↑ One of the better-known press photographs of the later second-generation Transporter and one of only a handful taken in colour.

second luggage space, the 1700 was compact in nature. The cooling fan was relocated from its traditional position at the top of the engine to the nose of the crankshaft at the rear. The fan was contained within a different style of housing, which conducted air over the engine through cleverly channelled ducts and led to more efficient cooling.

To accommodate what enthusiasts refer to as the 'suitcase' style of engine, the design of the Transporter's engine compartment was altered. The rear beam below the engine lid was now welded into position rather than being held in place by bolts that could be undone when the engine needed to come out, as had previously been the case. Although this change was only relevant to Transporters fitted with the new 1700 engine, the changed design affected all models.

Similarly, the neat crescent-shaped cooling vents tucked high on the rear quarter panels were enlarged, became rectangular in nature and were redesigned to make them stand proud of the surrounding metalwork. Together with one further change, the much larger rectangular rear light clusters already referred to, units so much bigger that they demanded a retooling of the adjoining metalwork, the visual appearance of the Transporter was changing. The following year would see more significant styling alterations and the emergence of the designation T2b. This rapidly led to 1972 model year examples, a blend of old and new, being called the 'crossover' Transporter by enthusiasts.

From the VW Camper owner's point of view, the most significant change made in August 1972 (for the '73 model year) was the creation of a fully fledged cab crumple zone, an invaluable improvement in the event of a head-on collision. In terms of practicality, Volkswagen cut a hole in the Transporter's luggage compartment, making access to the suitcase-style engine considerably easier. For those who prefer not to use their left leg when driving, the new-look model was also available as a three-speed automatic. At best, performance might be described as leisurely.

The most significant visible change was the replacement of the blade-style bumpers with heavy-duty sectional girder-like items at both the front and rear of the vehicle. Although more robust in appearance, and possibly less prone to damage during the course of parking manoeuvres, the new bumpers could not be described as crumple proof. The external cab steps disappeared, while the size of the VW roundel on the Transporter's front was much reduced for no obvious reason. Volkswagen argued that the relocation of the front indicators much higher on the front panel (at either end of the ventilation grille) was essentially a visibility issue. The new units were smaller than previously and square in design.

⬇ Part of the front cover of the 1978 US-market brochure entitled 'It's more fun to take the bus'. Later second-generation Transporter characteristics include indicators below the windscreen at either end of the ventilation grille, a smaller VW roundel, girder-style bumpers, cab steps no longer visible and larger air vents at the rear.

In August 1973, the 1700 engine was replaced by the 1,796cc, 68PS 1800 unit, which was purloined from the upgraded version of the VW 411, which had been carefully but ineffectively rebranded as the 412. Although maximum power had been boosted by only 2PS and the top speed had similarly increased by a mere 4mph to 82mph, the big advantage of the 1800 came with its significant additional torque (1700 – 81lb ft at 3,200rpm, 1800 – 92.4lb ft at 3,000rpm).

Would-be Camper owners contemplating the purchase of a rust-free import from the United States should be aware that, initially to meet the demands of California state legislation, Transporters destined for the sunshine territory were fitted with Bosch L-Jetronic fuel injection from August 1973 and that within a year this practice encompassed all vehicles destined for America.

↓ With a higher roof panel than its German counterpart, from 2005 the Brazilian Kombi was powered by a 1.4-litre water-cooled engine and, as a result, carried the disfiguring radiator grille on its front panel.

As far as the VW Camper goes, there is really only one further change worthy of mention during the remaining years of Bay production. This occurred in August 1975 when Volkswagen upgraded the larger engine specification to 2.0 litres. As the VW 412 had been consigned to history, on this occasion Volkswagen press-ganged the engine from the joint-project mid-engine sports car, the VW Porsche 914. The 1,970cc unit offered 70PS at 4,200rpm and, despite Volkswagen's official top speed being a conservative 79mph, most owners had little difficulty in achieving 90mph if the occasion arose.

Although German production of the second-generation Transporter came to an end in 1979 (the last example being paraded around the Hanover factory in October of that year), both the Brazilian and Mexican factories continued to produce their own versions. Mexican production eventually ground to a halt in 1995, while Brazilian manufacture continued unabated until the end of 2013. For the purpose of a VW Camper Buyers' Guide, to trace the history of these models before 2000 would be a fruitless exercise as few, if any, grace our roads. However, after this date a relatively swift trade grew in the UK, with the private company Danbury importing Brazilian Transporters and converting them to Campers. The 21st-century Brazilian Transporter features a slightly raised roof panel when compared to its German ancestor, bumpers more akin to the early pre-facelift Bay (but lacking the built-in cab-step arrangement) and mildly re-profiled doors. In November 2005, Brazil finally dispensed with air-cooling (their engine having been a 48PS 1600 for many years) when they borrowed the 78PS 1.4-litre, fuel-injected, water-cooled engine fitted to their Fox model (and available on certain VW Polos) and squeezed it into the Transporter's engine bay. Difficult to access as this sounds, thanks to the 'hatch' in the rear luggage area and the traditional engine lid, maintenance is relatively easy. These late-model Brazilian Transporters are instantly recognisable by a disfiguring radiator grille on their once-elegant front panels. However, Danbury, recognising the disappointment of enthusiasts, were clever and produced a 'cover' bearing a remarkable resemblance to a front-mounted spare wheel, a popular addition of the 1970s with some conversion companies.

↑ Volkswagen recorded the journey of the last Brazilian-built second-generation Transporter to a permanent home as part of the collection of notable VWs stored for posterity in Germany.

1979–1990/1992
THE THIRD-GENERATION VW CAMPER

The third-generation Transporter is probably the most complex of all the generations to summarise. It bridges the gap between the individualistic air-cooled technology and in-vogue retro appeal evident in its predecessors and what, for the foreseeable future, can be seen as modern-day, largely powerful and increasingly fuel-efficient vehicles of an entirely conventional nature.

On the drawing board when the new generation of VW Golfs,

THE THIRD-GENERATION VW CAMPER

Length: 4,600mm
Width: 1,845mm
Height: 1,950mm

(1979 Bus, dimensions vary slightly over the years and according to model. Note: Campers with an elevating roof will carry a greater height even with the roof down.)

Although largely similar in construction to the second-generation Transporter (body shell welded directly to the frame, twin box-section longitudinal members, supplemented by cross-members and outriggers), both the platform over the rear-mounted engine and the main 'loading/passenger/camper' area were closer to the ground. The platform over the engine compartment was lower by 145mm and the main floor by 100mm, resulting in an interior capacity increase of 40 per cent. The glass area was increased by 22 per cent, while rearward visibility was increased by 50 per cent.

Significantly, the T3 was a design generally well in advance of the safety regulations of the time.

Initially engines were air-cooled, being variants of the 1.6- and 2.0-litre units offered with the T3's predecessor in its later years. From 1981, these engines were supplemented by a 50PS diesel unit (borrowed from the VW Golf), a move that necessitated the fitting of a radiator and accompanying grille at the front of the vehicle. Towards the end of 1982, two water-cooled 1.9-litre petrol engines unique to the Transporter replaced the air-cooled offerings. The remaining years of T3 production saw the introduction of more powerful diesel and petrol water-cooled engines. Then 1985 saw the arrival of the 70PS turbocharged 1600 diesel engine, while the same year witnessed the debut of a 2.1-litre 112PS fuel-injected petrol engine with an alleged maximum speed of 94mph.

Passats and Polos were launched, the third-generation Transporter's appearance was at least partly in keeping with such cars, but its slab-sided, boxy, or even angular exterior is not necessarily embraced by today's buyers with the same enthusiasm as it predecessors.

Similarly, and most likely due to Volkswagen's struggle to balance the books after a period of first bad management and then heavy investment, it was initially endowed with what some opted to call elderly air-cooled technology. The advent of a sluggish diesel engine and then water-cooled, though hardly conventional, petrol engines was welcomed with open arms by some and loathed with unequalled venom by others. Whatever the engine, it was located at the rear of the vehicle, together with the driving wheels, both features seen variously as advantageous or as an unwelcome legacy. While some remained enamoured with the extra interior space alleged by such an arrangement, not to mention the absence of wasteful bonnet/body overhang demanded by a front-engine, front-wheel-drive vehicle, others bemoaned such an arrangement. The intrusive nature of an engine at the rear cramped rearward access, as had been the case with earlier generations, or, as was the situation with the new model, demanded the compromise of making the engine difficult to access under a concealed lid hacked into the rear loading area, in return for a higher-than-average loading platform. As a result, even today, there are those who would only consider purchase of the third-generation Transporter with an air-cooled engine. Conversely, those happy to luxuriate in the power afforded by the later petrol engines and the potential economy of some of the diesel offerings, might be equally tempted to purchase the more convenient fourth-, or even fifth-generation Transporter.

Few would be unwise enough to pronounce either the first- or the second-generation Transporters to be rust-free vehicles. Protecting metal from the effects of water, salt and the ravages of winter was not a priority of vehicle manufacturers during the 1950s, '60s or '70s. However, Volkswagen's well-intentioned thought of allocating some protection to the third-generation's bodywork has, many years later, proved detrimental. In the perceived wisdom of the day, Volkswagen filled the third-generation Transporter's seams with protective filler. Unfortunately, with advancing years, and particularly when paint or panels haven't received regular doses of wax polish, the filler contracts, allowing water ingress and rust to develop. (Better news though for present-day buyers and owners is that, with effect from August 1985, all T3 models were dip treated in the factory during the course of the manufacturing process.)

Having no-doubt unwittingly influenced someone new to the world of VW Transporters against the third-generation Transporter, it is important

NAME THAT VAN
– T3, T25, VANAGON, TRANSPORTER AND CARAVELLE

While the nicknames Splitty and Bay are in widespread use for the first- and second-generation Transporters respectively, the once often-heard term of 'Wedge' for the model produced from 1979 to 1990/2 is little used today, while the even more unflattering 'Brick' disappeared from the enthusiast's vocabulary several years ago.

Volkswagen themselves complicated the story by proffering a new name for the Transporter in America while, a few years into production, also changing brand tactic with respect to load-bearing and passenger-carrying models within the range. Similarly the behind-the-scenes designation for the Transporter was scrambled when British dealers preferred a different term to that of their European counterparts.

In summary then, the third-generation Transporter was known as the Vanagon in the United States, a concocted name encompassing a combination of 'van' and the US name for passenger-carrying vehicles 'station wagon'. US-market VW Campers based on the third-generation model lost the equally contrived term Campmobile, so beloved of earlier years, and instead became Vanagon Campers.

The term Caravelle originally applied to a limited edition, or concept, passenger-carrying Transporter with a particularly high level of trim, but by the time the 1983 model-year range was launched, the term had been applied to all European-market people carriers, while the latest executive vehicle was christened the Caravelle Carat. (In the USA, not wishing to lose the Vanagon name, the more luxurious models could be identified by the suffix GL.)

Most Camper manufacturers used the Delivery Van, or a basic window van without seats, as the basis for their conversions, although potential purchasers should be aware that some Caravelle-based models do exist.

If the first-generation Transporter was officially the T1 (not to be confused with the Type 1 Beetle) and its successor the T2 (more often referred to as a Type 2) then it follows that the third-generation model would be the T3. In mainland Europe this was indeed the case, but in Britain the dealer network appears to have been so shocked by the apparent deliberate attempt to retain air-cooled technology that they named the new vehicle the T25 (in other words, the type two and a half).

Nowadays it is common practice to refer to the fourth- and fifth-generation models as the T4 and T5 respectively, which has tended to reinforce usage of the term T3 in preference to T25. The designations T1 and T2 remain suitably obscure!

Finally, would-be buyers may also come across late left-hand-drive models emblazoned with a badge that reads 'Multivan'. As a treat to anticipate, this model is described under the section allocated to the T4, the period when it acquired true significance.

← A late model Vanagon Camper GL depicted on the cover of a 1990 brochure produced for the Canadian market.

to note that during the vehicle's lifetime VW Camper specifications moved forward in leaps and bounds. Some manufacturers added such facilities as a shower unit, others might have been content with a semi built-in loo and several looked at the gadgetry of efficient temperature control. All, including Westfalia, who upgraded to a model known as the Joker to coincide with the debut of the T3 Transporter and later developed the California and its even more deluxe counterpart, the Atlantic, were aware they had to progress. While chipboard and plywood had definitely succeeded solid wood, much more carefully planned design and the use of modern laminates made most VW Campers appear increasingly like an additional room of the family home.

Unlike its predecessors, the third-generation Transporter didn't undergo significant visual changes partway through its production run. With the exception of the appearance of the wheels on those at, or near, the top of the range, for by this time alloys had infiltrated the world of selected T3s, visual changes were more or less restricted to an increasing use of plastic. Such items as the bumpers and the air intakes in the upper rear quarter panels were among the most noticeable, while as the production run progressed both colour-coding plastic and melding the shape of the bumpers and external mirrors to the body of the vehicle was noticeable.

At the third-generation Transporter's front two features help to date the vehicle. All such models carry what at first glance appears to be

↑ Early third-generation Transporters can be identified by the lack of a second grille on the front panel, girder-style bumpers with small plastic end caps and a lack of plastic trim on the air vents towards the rear of the vehicle. (Cover image from a 1980 Danbury brochure.)

a radiator grille between the headlamps. In reality, this feature was designed to mask air intake or ventilation vents. However, with the arrival of the first diesel engine during 1981, a second smaller grille appeared below the first and this, of course, was the genuine item. During 1982 and a little way into the 1983 model year, all Transporters carried the second grille as water-cooled engines replaced the air-cooled units.

The second identifying feature, twin rectangular headlamps rather than single round ones, started life as an exclusive for the model known as the Caravelle Carat, another concept vehicle that with effect from September 1985 became a standard model of the range. Towards the end of the production run, twin rectangular headlamps had filtered down to such basic models as the Delivery Van, which by this time was frequently the base model for a Camper conversion.

Roughly halfway through the production run of the third-generation Transporter, Volkswagen added an extra dimension with the introduction of 'syncro' models with permanent four-wheel drive.

With amended running gear ensuring power was directed to the rear axle and, via a prop shaft and viscous coupling, to the front axle, the driving force could be directed evenly to the front and rear wheels as required. The syncro concept was to prove popular (the use of a small 's' was integral to Volkswagen's branding) so that it was not unusual to find VW Camper conversions with an off-road capability. When general third-generation Transporter production ended in 1990, syncro models continued to be available for a further two years.

One further T3 story warrants at least a footnote. This relates to South Africa and production at the Uitenhage factory. Reluctant for once to follow in the footsteps of Hanover, when Germany turned to the all-new T4, Volkswagen of South Africa responded by giving the T3 a makeover and, most significantly, introduced the Audi fuel-injected, five-cylinder engine in three guises (2.3, 2.5 and 2.6 litre) to power the vehicle. Larger, vented disc brakes at the front ensured that the T3 could be brought to a rapid halt despite its increased performance. Other changes, apart from a slightly revised dashboard, included an increase in the size of the side windows (so that they encroached further down the body of the vehicle), black trim below the windscreen (to give the illusion of a greater area of glass), rear-facing vents in the air scoop and a redesigned upper and lower grille at the front (the latter extending to the full width of the vehicle and incorporating the indicators). Production of this modified T3 continued at Uitenhage until 2002.

⬇ This cover illustration from the 1984 Autohomes brochure clearly shows how, once water-cooled engines were installed in the T3, a second grille became a feature of the Camper's front end.

1990–2003
THE FOURTH-GENERATION VW CAMPER

Predictably, when Volkswagen launched the T4, dealers were armed with a lengthy inventory of reasons to purchase the new model. Sifting through and rejecting any assets attributable to the vehicle simply because it was a Volkswagen the list simplifies to four key points:

Front-wheel drive with good general driving stability – even in difficult situations – independent suspension remained an essential ingredient of the T4's make-up (front: torsion bars, upper and lower wishbones, anti-roll bar; rear: mini coil springs, semi-trailing arms) as did disc brakes at the front. From 1996, and as part of the 'long-nose' upgrade, disc brakes also became the norm at the rear. Likewise, standard to T4s powered by the VR6 engine but otherwise an optional extra, combined ABS and traction control made the vehicle safer. Volkswagen was also proud to note the vehicle's 'safety cell construction' (enhanced from 1996), which included side-impact protection.

Aerodynamically favourable short bonnet concept with both good cab position and visibility – the drag coefficient of the T4 stood at 0.36 compared to the T3's 0.44. Factors included rounded contours of the frontal design, windows that bonded flush with the outer shell, the

⬇ 'Take a look at the new Caravelle' proclaims the message accompanying this image of the launch-year T4 – the first Transporter with both a bonnet and a long-wheelbase option.

THE FOURTH-GENERATION VW CAMPER

The fourth-generation Transporter was the first to be offered in short- and long-wheelbase versions:

Length: (Short wheelbase, 2,920mm) 4,655mm; (Long wheelbase 3,320mm) 5,055mm
Width: 1,845mm
Height: 1,940mm

(1992 Delivery Vans. Note: Campers with an elevating roof will carry a greater height even with the roof down.)

From January 1996, two styles of T4 were available. Workhorse models retained the short nose of earlier examples but benefitted from new moulded bumpers, while passenger-carrying T4s featured a redesigned bonnet and frontal appearance (including re-profiled bumpers) to accommodate the bulk of the new VR6 petrol engine (and 2.5TDI diesel unit). Although the terminology is unofficial, most know the two styles of T4s as short- or long-nose models.

Length:
Short-nose Transporter with later profile bumpers: 4,707mm
Short-wheelbase, long-nose Caravelle: 4,789mm
Long-wheelbase, long-nose Caravelle: 5,189mm

As had been widely anticipated, the fourth-generation Transporter broke the mould of previous models by being entirely conventional in nature; it was a vehicle that, when de-badged, could easily have been mistaken for a Ford, Vauxhall or any of the myriad versions produced by countless manufacturers. That the T4 retained a significant following for Volkswagen is testament to build quality, after-sales service and, ultimately, an ability to capitalise on strong resale values.

Within the confines of a conventional design, nevertheless, the lifespan of the T4 can be divided into two segments. Although predictably sought after before 1996, it was only with the long-nose models, already referred to, that the T4 became genuinely powerful (with the introduction of the VR6 petrol engine) and both economical and powerful following the debut of the 2.5TDI diesel engine at the same time. Later succeeded by the even more powerful V6 engine, the VR6 offered a top speed of 109mph, its successor being capable of 120mph. The 2.5TDI, Volkswagen asserted, offered a top speed of a respectable 98mph, although many found it capable of much more, while an average fuel consumption of 35.8mpg was scarcely believable compared to what had been the norm previously.

Although T4 Campers inevitably lack the retro appeal of the first- and second-generation models, they have a considerable following, a fan base that extends beyond the realms of battalions of VW enthusiasts to the wider camping fraternity.

absence of rain channels and the inclusion of recessed door handles). Cab creature comforts were enhanced in 1996 when all models received a new-style dashboard, which was much more in tune with saloon styles than had been the case ever since the Transporter's debut nearly half a century earlier. Airbags were offered for the driver and front passenger, while the cab was also better sound insulated.

Engine installed transversely at the front, allowing a completely level load area at the rear, or the cab/chassis frame arrangement ideal for special bodies – old-school diehards were quick to point out that a short-wheelbase T4 Delivery Van offered 4.0m² of floor load area, while the T3 owner benefitted from 4.36m². However, a long-wheelbase T4 afforded an extravagant 4.62m² of space!

Front axle located well to the front facilitating comfortable access to the vehicle's cab. Additionally, and a big asset for current day owners, was the level of anti-corrosion treatment employed, which included bitumen wax undersealing and cavity protection. Volkswagen was eager to declare that:

'*The patented hot wax flooding method is a first in commercial vehicle manufacture worldwide and absolutely unique up to now. ...*'

⬇ The long-nose T4, seen here in syncro guise and hence the photographer's choice of setting.

To complement this method, and the attendant six-year guarantee against rusting through, the T4 had been built in a way that minimised possible rust traps, a method of construction that involved both 'open profiles' and 'large metal parts without joints'.

Finally and no doubt in part an answer to the lack of engine accessibility afforded with the T3, the T4's designers engineered a way of manoeuvring both the radiator and its associated grille forward by 100mm by simply loosening a few screws and pulling a handle.

⬆ The long-nose T4 Multivan – to all outward appearances just another Caravelle but in reality a most useful and practical addition to any family's collection of vehicles.

A NOTE CONCERNING THE US VERSION OF THE T4 – THE EUROVAN

While some cynics might suggest that the chosen name of EuroVan was a primary cause of the T4's less-than-successful story in the USA, the truth of the matter is that Volkswagen of America generally had reached rock bottom. The EuroVan was debuted at the Boston Auto Show in late 1991, but it was another 12 months before very limited supplies became available, largely due to exclusive US-specification issues. In 1993, Volkswagen sold a paltry 49,533 vehicles in the USA and as the operation struggled to regenerate itself, the EuroVan no longer appeared on the list of vehicles available the following year. After an absence of six years, the EuroVan returned to the US market, available as a GLS (Caravelle) or MV (Multivan Camper).

2003–2015
THE FIFTH-GENERATION VW CAMPER

Volkswagen's own California oozed quality and refinement, although its specification and particularly its lack of gadgetry might have led some to regard it as relatively basic, particularly when compared to the luxurious conversions offered by some of the well-known names of today. (Volkswagen was also criticised in some UK quarters for presenting a conversion still geared to a left-hand-drive vehicle – the sliding side door opened on the driver's side of the vehicle, whereas for the home market the more camper/safety friendly passenger side was offered. Obviously able to produce side-loading doors geared to right-hand-drive vehicles, Volkswagen must have deemed it not financially viable to rework the interior for such an orientation.

Perhaps at this point, it should also be mentioned that the variety of California options was severely limited in Great Britain. However,

THE FIFTH-GENERATION VW CAMPER

The fifth-generation Transporter was the first to be offered as a Camper built at the factory by Volkswagen. The California offered to the British market was a short-wheelbase model. Both long-wheelbase and high-top versions were available in Germany. Please note the T5 was not part of the range in the USA.

The fifth-generation Transporter generally was offered in short- and long-wheelbase versions, while three roof heights were also offered.

The range was given a facelift with effect from September 2009, while a new range of common-rail diesel engines were claimed to be considerably more efficient than the outgoing 'Pumpe Duese' (PD) technology units they replaced.

Length:
(Short wheelbase as quoted for the VW California, 3,000mm) 4,890mm
(Long-wheelbase 3,400mm) 5,290mm
Width: 1,904mm (excluding door mirrors)

Height:
California 1,990mm,
Window Van with low roof 1,969mm,
Window Van with medium roof 2170mm

From September 2009, the face-lifted VW California had a quoted overall length of 4,892mm, width 1,904mm (excluding door mirrors) and an overall height of 1,995mm. The overall length of long-wheelbase models increased by 2mm to 5,292mm.

anyone happy to contemplate a left-hand-drive vehicle would be able to consider a solid high-roof version, the equivalent of the Multivan (now renamed the California Beach and latterly available in the UK) and trim levels that included both the so-called Trendline and Comfortline.

However, for the purpose of this summary, the British-market California SE (SE in VW trim level terms standing for middle-of-the-road) is used as the basis for illustrating, as you might expect, that the fifth-generation Transporter carried a level of technical sophistication above that of its predecessor. Possibly more important still, the fifth-generation Transporter confirmed the supremacy and economy of diesel (particularly for a vehicle of this size) appropriate to the greener, leaner years of the new millennium.

A snippet from launch-era literature is sufficient to tell the tale: 'The California is extremely sure footed – high body rigidity, large anti-roll bars, MacPherson suspension struts and independent rear suspension combine to ensure a dynamic driving experience. Safety is paramount to Volkswagen, which is why Anti-lock Brake System (ABS), Electronic Differential Lock (EDL), Traction Control

⬇ A deluxe version of the T5 as launched in March 2003, its car-like frontal appearance bearing a similarity to Volkswagen cars of the era including the Passat B5, Golf Mk4 and Bora.

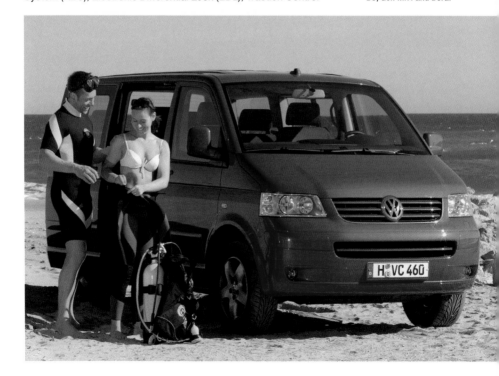

↑ The T5 as it was launched in California guise – note that this press image betrays the model's potential defect: the layout is essentially geared to a left-hand-drive model with the side-loading door spilling happy campers straight onto the road.

System (TCS), Engine Braking Control (EBC), Electronic Stabilisation Programme (ESP) not to mention driver, passenger, side and front curtain airbags all come as standard.'

Alternatively, on the subject of the advance of the tin-worm, while the T4 was leaps and bounds ahead of the earlier generations, it was subsequently eclipsed by its successor. First then, an extract from material published at the time when the long-nose T4 made its debut:

'Volkswagen was the first volume manufacturer to offer a six-year warranty to cover against internal corrosion. Special rust-proofing treatment of internal body sections and panels, applied at the time of manufacture, guards against through-rusting from the inside ...'

A decade later, with the T5, Volkswagen could proclaim that, 'the internal body sections and panels of the California are covered against rusting through from the inside for 12 years ... .'

The British-market T5 California at launch and before the model was face-lifted could be purchased with a choice of two diesel engines, plus either a manual or automatic gearbox and for would-be campers avoiding Chelsea High Street, Volkswagen's all-wheel drive system, branded 4MOTION. As with the Transporter, as opposed to Caravelle options, a petrol engine was not available, although no doubt someone somewhere will have created a Camper out of a Caravelle endowed with the 235PS V6 petrol engine coupled to a six speed auto 'box. (Similarly, there are undoubtedly Campers out and about powered by either the 85PS or 104PS 1.9TDI engines as offered on some delivery and window-style vans.) Key to the options on offer, and the only choices for prospective California owners, were the 130PS and 174PS 2.5TDI engines. The former, Volkswagen claimed, took 16.3 seconds to reach 62mph from a standing start, the latter a competitive 13.0 seconds. Top speeds of 103 and 115mph (112mph for the 174PS Tiptronic, or auto-box, and the 4MOTION options) revealed the California/T5 to be no sluggard. Significantly, the trend of decent fuel economy, established by the 2.5-litre, 102PS TDI installed in the T4 in the mid-1990s, continued, with combined totals calculated at 33.6mpg for the 130PS engine and 32.8mpg for the 174PS option, both fitted with a manual 6-speed gearbox.

The negatives and positives of the appearance of Volkswagen's T5 facelift of late 2009 are essentially a matter of personal preference. If the latest corporate style offered by Volkswagen on models from the Polo to the Touareg appeals more than that afforded cars such as the Mk4 Golf and B5.5 Passat, then the face-lifted T5 will endear itself more than the vehicle as it was launched.

⬇ The facelift
T5 California.

↑ The facelift T5 of late 2009 vintage and onwards with a representative from each preceding generation of Transporter.

Of greater significance though is the move away from Pumpe Duese technology to common-rail engines. A short extract from contemporary literature paints the larger picture:

'Our renowned TDI engines have long been setting the standards in diesel technology – and with rising fuel costs, we've also been working hard to lower fuel consumption, while reducing CO_2 emissions. The California range reflects this with a choice of three 2.0-litre common-rail diesel engines, all complying with Euro 5 emission limits and equipped with diesel particulate filters as standard. Two of the engines use TDI technology, while the powerful 180PS diesel engine features BiTurbo (BiTDI) technology for the ultimate diesel experience. On the California Beach, there's a choice of 114PS or 140PS TDI diesel engines, while the SE offers either the 140PS TDI or the more powerful 180PS BiTDI twin-

turbo diesel engine. And when mated to a choice of 5 or 6-speed manual, or 7-speed dual-clutch direct shift (DSG) gearboxes, you'll discover our engines will carry you to your destination swiftly and smoothly.'

Two final points pertaining to the face-lifted T5 conclude this introduction to the near 65-year history of eclipsed models. First, mention should be made of BlueMotion Technology. In keeping with the endeavours of other manufacturers, Volkswagen added cruise control, low-rolling-resistance tyres, regenerative braking (as you brake the alternator turns and the battery charges) and start/stop technology, under the umbrella of BMT with the aim of further improving fuel consumption and reducing CO_2 emissions. Second, hot on the heels of the facelift, Volkswagen in the UK opted to carry the Multivan-style California Beach as part of the range.

CHAPTER 2
PRIMARY USAGE –
MARKS OUT OF TEN

Assuming that when you bought this book you knew little or nothing about VW Campers, providing you have read and digested the previous chapter, you should have more than an inkling concerning the first five generations of Transporter/Camper. Hopefully, if your knowledge of the VW Camper was already reasonable, the résumé will have acted as a useful refresher.

The task here is to help you choose which generation you wish to investigate further based on what you have learned so far. Primary usage is the key consideration. To help the decision process, a rudimentary scoring system has been added, albeit subjective and defined by the author's personal preferences based on books researched and painstakingly written, concours models judged and the stories related by many owners over the years. A score of ten suggests the model is as near perfect as possible, anything meriting five or above worth investigating at least, while everything below a five requires a great deal of thought and justification on your part.

⬇ A T4 1990s
Auto-Sleeper Trooper
– ideal for weekends
away and holidays.

Five main categories are easy to identify although the practised VW Camper owner might well suggest that the borders between each should be conveniently blurred.

1   A daily driver, covering commuting to work, delivering and collecting the kids from school, supermarket trolley runs and of course weekend outings and even holidays in the UK and abroad.

2   A second vehicle, used more-or-less exclusively for relaxing weekends and holiday adventures.

3   A second vehicle designed to qualify you as a card-carrying member of the VW community, involving club activities, weekend gatherings and attendance at a reasonable number of the many shows held through the spring, summer and autumn, definitely in Britain and possibly across Europe.

4   A second, or even third, vehicle in original or restored condition designed to be a show exhibit/concours queen at the many events held in Britain and Europe.

5   Cheating slightly, a garage project, where the fun is in the restoration rather than the finished product. This category will include vehicles intended for resale when work has been completed.

⬆ A good solid second-generation Camper – probably the best of the bunch for budding card-carrying members of the VW community.

1 DAILY DRIVER

Realistically, the newer the vehicle the more likely it is to be suitable as a daily driver. Clearly, a brand new VW Camper, straight from the showroom, will attract the highest score (providing your budget stretches to this level of expense). A T5 will also be ideal (assuming you are happy that your purchase price today and the vehicle's resale value for the foreseeable future will probably not equate to each other). A later model T4, preferably endowed with the 2.5TDI engine, could be a wise choice for a few more years (as depreciation is hardly rampant and longevity seems assured).

Considering that all examples of the generations before the T4 must be at least a quarter of a century old, common sense suggests daily driver status to be unrealistic. Admittedly, a rejuvenated and carefully customised/modernised example might be able to keep pace with today's high-tech cars, but considering the amount likely to have been spent to achieve such an ambition, few will be eager to watch the salt and general detritus of winter roads eat into their pride and joy.

⬇ The T4 makes a practical daily driver.

SUITABILITY AS A DAILY DRIVER

FIRST-GENERATION TRANSPORTER   1–2
No, no, no! The exception to the rule of 'for summer use only' might be a first-generation Transporter with a big engine, 12-volt electrics and a disc-brake conversion.

SECOND-GENERATION TRANSPORTER   1–5
Don't do it! Daily drivers do exist. But think about it. If it's original, the salt of successive winters will ruin it. If it's restored and upgraded, you might as well light your fire with a five-pound note each day! Daily use, summer only, or buy a Brazilian Bay for similar reasons.

T3   3–4
1979 or 1989 vintage as a daily driver isn't something many would envisage. Banger status possibly, but you will be lucky to find anything decent at a banger price!

T4   6–8 (BUT THE LATER THE BETTER)
Examples produced towards the end of the production run are still seen in daily use. Would you consider another vehicle dating from the early 1990s as suitable for the day-in, day-out rigors of this category?

T5   10
Even the oldest examples date from a similar period to many of the cars you see in daily usage.

➜ Inevitably top marks go to the T5.

2 SUMMER WEEKENDER, HOLIDAY ADVENTURER

The older the VW Camper the less likely it is to appeal to you if your one aim in life is to go camping at weekends and luxuriate in as many holidays as possible. Similarly, apart from Volkswagen's reputation as a provider of reliable, quality products, presumably the freedom linked to larger vehicles and the enviable gadgetry associated with Camper conversions based on other marques could well be a big draw. Realistically, price might also play its part, for not only are Volkswagen models perceived to be expensive in the first place but also their popularity ensures a higher resale value.

However, assuming that the Volkswagen's particular type of magic has begun to work (and in the future may mean that you head-off into the territory of category three), probably the most important section

⬇ The T4 Gatcombe from Auto-Sleepers, luxury weekends and holidays in the UK and beyond.

SUITABILITY AS A SUMMER WEEKENDER OR HOLIDAY ADVENTURER

FIRST-GENERATION TRANSPORTER   1–2

Unless you have mechanical knowledge, or the vehicle has been radically updated, a Splitty isn't for you. Yes, it has all the kudos of in-vogue retro appeal, but an original interior is seriously museum like, while you will pay a great deal of money for a customised exterior/interior that may or may not hold its value.

SECOND-GENERATION TRANSPORTER   4–5 (8)

Almost as sought after as its predecessor and carrying nearly as much retro charm, some of the later models are bordering on non-enthusiast practicality (particularly if you can cope with LHD). A 2.0-litre engine is reasonably powerful (although you might still have a queue behind you), but it is also thirsty. Numbers available (at a price) are sufficient to acquire an original interior, which might be preferable to something bespoke created by the previous owner. What scores 8? A Brazilian Bay – a vehicle built recently, with a modern water-cooled engine (and probably converted by a firm in the UK). Note its origins though and resultant lack of original rust protection.

T3   2–3

Why would you buy this generation? It hasn't got the retro appeal, yet it is old. In its favour though, it won't cost a fortune to purchase (but it will do when the rust breaks out), and a late model diesel won't be too thirsty. Best of all, assuming it's in good condition, Camper interiors were starting to acquire more of the conveniences associated with modern living.

T4   7–8

Styling of the later long-nose models is convincingly attractive and as yet, doesn't look unduly dated. Original spec conversions usually offer both life's little luxuries and materials that have worn well. Layouts offer a degree of sophistication over and above anything produced previously. In addition, this is the first generation with its engine at the front, thus affording the opportunity to create a Motorhome-style body, which had been difficult to achieve previously. If your budget is okay but hardly overflowing, this might be a better bet than a T5. Depreciation on early Camper models is still apparent but not drastic, but this is not the case for some of the luxurious conversions of later years.

T5   8–9

Short of buying a brand new model and having sufficient in the coffers to cover the cost, the T5 has to be the best bet. Performance is spot-on, whether it's Common Rail or Pumpe Duese technology, while economy is also difficult to fault. Interiors are suave and sophisticated. There is only one drawback to T5 ownership, and the newer the model, the worse it is. Depreciation is rife and is likely to be noticeable for a good few years to come.

⬆ The 'suitability' scoring system suggests a second-generation Camper isn't the ideal weekender or holiday vehicle. However, there are companies who hire out such vehicles for just such reasons. Worth a thought?

of this book will be the one devoted to the manufacturers and brands of approved conversions linked to the T5 or T4. The purchase of a customised model, with fancy wheels, additional trim, spectacular but possibly bizarre paint jobs and a magnificent sound system isn't going to be for you.

One point to mention, which has been more-or-less overlooked so far, and particularly relevant here, is the elevating roof, or possibly a fixed high top. Both ensure long-lasting impersonations of Quasimodo-like characters are avoidable although it's only the high-top owners that pay the price of not being able to access a variety of car parks.

Finally, a word of warning to the potential owner who realises that he or she falls into this category. Don't be taken in by the chocolate-box prettiness and craving for all things from the 1950s, 1960s and at least part of the 1970s. Trust the many voices of experience: a first- or second-generation Transporter converted into a Camper is not for you.

3 A MEMBER OF THE VW CAMPER COMMUNITY

While a 1500 engine first-generation VW Camper, with for example an SO42 Westfalia interior or a Devon Caravette conversion, is likely to be more than fit for purpose, a Bay should really offer more. Dependent on the 'breed' of conversion selected, the second-generation VW Camper will present a more convenient and comfortable layout, more engine power, while retaining well over 90 per cent of the in-vogue nostalgia appeal.

At the moment, possibly the third-generation VW Camper is the least exciting of the versions on offer. Its 1980s styling lacks the appeal of its predecessors, while, when compared to its successors, it falls short in terms of specification. Diehard air-cooled enthusiasts will be restricted to an early-model T3 and will be pushed inevitably in the direction of the least underpowered option, namely the 2.0-litre engine. The advent of both diesel and water-cooled petrol engines might suggest a big step forward, but in both instances performance could well be deemed pedestrian. The argument follows that while permanent slow-lane driving is acceptable with a 'fun' vehicle – terminology appropriate to both first- and second-generation models – this is less likely to appeal to would-be T3 owners. Of course, later vehicles sported more powerful, if relatively thirsty, engines, while there is a fraternity who regard the permanent four-wheel-drive T3, branded as the syncro, as the ultimate VW Camper.

⬇ Okay, it would be impolite to exclude the first-generation Camper from the Camper community category.

↑ Your colour scheme, your updates and a bigger engine. Ideal for many a VW community member.

In terms of Camper conversions, inevitably a mid-1980s layout is going to be of a higher specification than that of a vehicle produced 10 or 20 years earlier. The magpie's desire for ever shinier gadgetry, keep-warm, stay-cool temperatures, cook-this, chill-that technology, was rife, but, and to many it's a big but, all was melded together in a package that nowadays simply oozes undesirable fads and fashion. One day such styles will return to the podium, but they haven't yet.

If vintage or retro is deemed impractical, possibly crawling about underneath the vehicle has lost its adventurous appeal, and it isn't important that your Camper sports a more recent registration plate, the T4 must rank highly as a suitable vehicle for following the VW crowd while indulging in latter-day luxury. Entirely conventional in its design – front-wheel-drive, engine fore of the cab – many of the later examples with a stock interior could almost have rolled straight out of the showroom. There is absolutely no reason why slow-lane motoring should be anything other than your choice. The 2.5TDI engine of the mid/late 1990s can be regarded as one of the first modern diesels to appeal to van and car drivers alike. If fuel consumption isn't high on the agenda – after all this is a purely-for-pleasure T4 – then you could revel in either the VR6 or V6 petrol engines, which are powerful units indeed.

For the moment at least, internal styling remains not only serviceable but reasonably fashionable, while externally it is hard to fault the appearance of the T4, and particularly so the so-called long-nose models, which ran alongside the original frontal design from the mid/late 1990s.

Everything already said in relation to the T4 is predictably also

applicable to an original/stock T5. While many families will be more than happy to drive a car that is five or ten years old, few would think their means of transport appropriate if it had been built in the early 1990s. Similarly, the diesel Pumpe Duese engines (literally unit injector), which powered the T5 until late 2009, can be regarded as both powerful and economical. However, the new generation of common-rail diesels can both outperform them and rack up an even higher score in the economy stakes. The biggest downside to T5 ownership will, of course, be depreciation, but even here, selection of a model from the earlier years of the production run will ensure less of an impact in this respect.

A significant complication arises in the VW Camper enthusiast category. While it is easy to discount the earlier vehicles as everyday drivers and possibly to question some of the Camper conversions of the late 1950s and early 1960s as bordering on impractical even for an enthusiast, any generation with a modern conversion and possibly an upgraded engine, fits the criteria for summer weekend/holiday use. Indeed, this could easily be where the first-generation Transporter scores most highly. Similarly, the Bay isn't far behind, while some might even suggest it has the edge. Both certainly tick all the 'visually appealing' and 'desirable' boxes and if upgraded become entirely practical for charging across the country in pursuit of the VW passion.

Here's the list. Externally, there is no restriction on what colour scheme you choose for your first- or second-generation Camper and should you want to add decals, there is no rule written to say you can't. You may also opt to adorn the vehicle with anything from a vintage-style

⬆ Does the T4 fit the VW community member bill? Of course it does and it is popular too.

↑ T3 fans, remember if you are going to join Club 80–90, a later model is less likely to suffer tin-worm issues. Why not go all the way and enjoy off-road fun with the syncro?

roof rack to headlight 'eyebrows'. You might opt to chrome bumpers that once were painted, while the fitting of one style of the many 'posh' wheels available will help to create the vehicle's unique identity.

Many prefer to lower the ride height from that prescribed by Volkswagen and greatly improve stopping power via the addition of disc brakes (both front and rear). Lift the engine lid at the rear and it's odds-on that you will have selected to upgrade the engine from its original specification (perhaps not if your vehicle is a later model Bay already endowed with a 1.8- or 2.0-litre lump). 'Big' air-cooled engines are readily available, while some opt to crowbar in offerings from other manufacturers, most notably in this instance, Subaru.

Inside, the choice is entirely yours. You may opt to create a modern take on a classic real-wood interior from the 1950s or 1960s, or, like many with an older house, you could easily select a contemporary makeover. Nor does it end there. Some are keen to cram as many units in as possible leaving sleeping accommodation somewhat restricted, while others take Volkswagen's Multivan approach and keep units to the bare essentials. That's the beauty of a van not destined to take centre stage on the concours circuit – you can please yourself, and in so doing rightly claim that 'home is where you park it'.

SUITABILITY FOR VW CLUB MEMBERS AND ENTHUSIAST BRIGADE

FIRST-GENERATION TRANSPORTER   8–10

An ideal vehicle for those already hooked by the VW fisherman. Assuming total originality, or costly restoration to achieve the closest you can get to such status, isn't your thing, a sound-bodied first-generation Transporter could still be your ideal vehicle. Repaint it in your favourite hue, create an interior that ticks all the boxes you desire, lower it a shade, add a bigger engine (air or water-cooled) and discs all round and you are going to make many green with envy, and receive lots of admiring glances.

SECOND-GENERATION TRANSPORTER   9–10 (6)

With virtually the same level of retro appeal as its predecessor, but always likely to cost a little less, you will have more power in standard form and the option to select an original interior ahead of anything offered on a first-generation Transporter. On the other hand, all that can be done to a Splitty model to make it your own can be applied to a Bay just as easily. Possibly, the earlier models lend themselves more to the retro dream. What scores a 6? The Brazilian lookalikes dating from the new millennium.

T3   6–8

Less expensive to purchase than an earlier generation model and these days, with a reasonable following, the T3 lacks the retro appeal of its predecessors. Many would argue that the early 2.0-litre air-cooled engine is the best option, but later diesels with turbo power have their supporters. More generously proportioned than its predecessors, a standard conversion will also offer luxuries not available to owners of earlier models.

T4   8–9

Both the T4 and the T5 have a big following among those who regard a first- or second-generation Transporter as simply too old and impractical. In standard form, Camper conversions are appropriately in keeping with modern-day requirements. If you spend a great deal of money on creating (or having someone create) a bespoke interior, don't necessarily expect to recoup all your money if you come to sell. Considering that, there would be little point in buying a fully fledged Camper, only to start from scratch in creating your vision – the best option could well be a Delivery Van, Window Van or Kombi.

T5   6–9

The big question here is: how old does a vehicle have to be before it's ripe for customising? If your passion is originality and a decent conversion without paying the second-mortgage numbers required for a brand new VW Camper then varying ages according to budget of T5 might be for you. If you want to go for a lowered look, with a bespoke state-of-the-art interior, you will have to indulge your hobby at the expense of your wallet.

4 SHOW EXHIBIT/ CONCOURS QUEEN

First, a few definitions are necessary. Concours competitions can be divided into two categories: one a remarkably serious business judged by an expert on the model presented for assessment, the other a 'show and shine', usually marked by either an enthusiast told to pick his or her personal favourite, or all those showing their vehicles. Entrants are similarly divided, although one further category of individual exits. This is dedicated to the owners who are eager to present their vehicle in as immaculate a manner as possible, ensuring originality or correct-to-the-year parts, but who don't want their vehicles pawed over by a judge, or ranked against others of a similar nature. These are the relatively large band of individuals who opt to drive and display their vehicles, often

CONCOURS D'ELEGANCE

Item	Aspects to be considered	Points
Paintwork and panels	Originality, freedom from damage, original colour	/20
Exterior trim	Completeness, freedom from damage, originality	/20
Wheels and tyres	Cleanliness, freedom from damage, five identical tyres of correct size, wheels original type/colour	/20
Under-body	Cleanliness, freedom from damage and rust, obvious signs of welding	/20
Interior	Cleanliness, no tears or excessive wear, correct functioning of parts, originality	/20
Luggage compartment	Originality, cleanliness, tool kit complete, freedom from damage	/20
Engine compartment	Originality and cleanliness, including underside	/20
	Subtotal	/140
Penalty Points	Not licensed for road use or brought to the event by trailer	Deduct 10 points
	Ill-fitting or unsuitable accessories	Deduct up to 10 points
	Total	

← Hardly suitable as a Camper but this Campahome from Moortown Motors of 1963 vintage is ideal material for Concours d'Elegance trophies.

travelling considerable distances to do so and who invariably enjoy every minute of what is usually a vintage experience.

Let's be honest, to use a potential concours-winning VW Camper regularly would either demand such an extraordinary amount of care as to make a weekend away positively unpleasant, or would result in a deterioration of the vehicle likely to deprive it and its pernickety owner of shiny trophies. On that basis it appears logical to suggest that the older the VW Camper bought for such purposes the better, at least as far as classic Concours d'Elegance go. Most show organisers will not yet have created a class for the T5, while entries for the T4 (if not combined with the T3) tend to be well down on those of the early generations.

Most classic concours judges (whatever the judging sheet might suggest) will favour a totally original vehicle over a 'restored to original condition' vehicle, while correctly penalising anything that could be regarded as incorrect for the year.

↑ Seen at a vintage VW gathering held at Hessisch Oldendorff, Germany every four years.

Realistically, there aren't that many people who will deliberately buy a concours-condition Camper. The cost will be high, possibly even excessive and once purchased it cannot be used for the purpose for which it was originally created.

When it comes to the field of the custom concours, this is a slightly different matter. Generally, although not exclusively, the more extreme the customisation, the more money ploughed into the project, the greater chance an owner has of coming away with a trophy. Expensive metallic or pearlescent paint jobs, wider wheels, a lowered stance, bigger and highly chromed engines (on earlier models) are all likely to attract higher ratings than a straightforward and no doubt more practical bespoke interior.

It would seem unwise for a custom fan to buy a vehicle that has already undergone the full treatment, while it might well be a dubious move for someone who has built a personalised camping interior for weekend and holiday use to enter a custom concours only to find that their taste doesn't coincide with that of the judge.

If you are contemplating parting with a considerable sum in order to partake in Concours d'Elegance competitions, the judging sheet on page 54, compiled from several of the most demanding events on the calendar, should both assist in your selection and illustrate that a good judge will be particularly finicky.

SHOW EXHIBIT/CONCOURS QUEEN

FIRST-GENERATION TRANSPORTER   10 (ORIGINAL) 8 (CUSTOM)

You will pay a great deal of money to buy either an original VW Camper or a fully restored model to show. However, rest assured, you are likely to get your money back if you decide to sell. Customised first-generation Transporters are slightly more risky, but only because preferences are always of an individual nature and, what you really liked when you bought the vehicle, might not appeal to others.

SECOND-GENERATION TRANSPORTER   10 (ORIGINAL) 8 (CUSTOM)

Essentially, the words devoted to the first-generation model can be repeated here with one slight variation. You will pay a goodly sum for a second-generation Camper but not as much as for its predecessor.

T3   5 (ORIGINAL) 6 (CUSTOM)

The newer the Transporter the fewer the classic concours events to include a class for your pride and joy – hence the score. Reserving a T3, T4 or T5 for concours events and very little else, and finding yourself lumped in with two more generations of Transporter and facing perhaps a maximum of two or three other vehicles, can hardly be a rewarding experience. Custom concours is definitely better, but the T3 isn't a favourite.

T4 AND T5   3 (ORIGINAL) 8 (CUSTOM)

The comments have already been made concerning classic concours and later VW Campers. However, both the T4 and T5 lend themselves to a combination of weekend usage (to attend shows) and custom concours events. However, be committed to spending money on a host of props to concours triumph (and outpacing your fellows) and the knowledge that you won't get your money back. Also with the T5, more so than the T4, you face depreciation on the vehicle.

➡ Custom concours winner lined-up with at least one fellow trophy holder.

5 GARAGE PROJECT

To bracket a 'garage project' with the term 'primary usage' clearly doesn't make sense, but there are those who get more enjoyment and sense of achievement out of the restoration process than when driving or camping in the finished vehicle. Logically, the older and rarer the Camper (or Transporter) to be worked on, the more difficult new panels and parts are to acquire, the greater the complexity of the project, and the more all-embracing will be the feeling of accomplishment when the vehicle is finished.

Although for the true garage-project enthusiast the process will be a labour of love, the particularly canny will also have an eye firmly on the cost of the vehicle shell, the inevitable monies spent during the course of the restoration, the predicted selling price and the maximum profit achievable. Suddenly, budgets and investment potential have become topics for urgent analysis.

⬇ Coming along nicely – restoration project seen at Bus Types show, 2013.

GARAGE PROJECT

FIRST-GENERATION TRANSPORTER   10
While even a rust bucket won't be available for a song, and the parts for a full restoration are likely to cost a great deal, the potential reward if the purpose is to sell will make it all worthwhile. If the intention is to keep the Camper for the foreseeable future, you can rest assured that if you do decide to sell, you are likely to recoup your investment and make some more.

SECOND-GENERATION TRANSPORTER   9
Second-generation Transporters ripe for restoration are still readily available. Of course, sellers will be aware of the value of even rusty examples, but it should be possible to find something sounder than the equivalent first-generation model. Parts and panels are available, at a cost of course, and you might have to be a little bit more careful with your outgoings if your intention is to sell and reap a reward. If the plan is to keep the restored vehicle, be reassured that prices continue to climb!

T3   4.5
While it's true that T3 prices are gradually moving in an upwards direction, the chances of recouping your money following a ground-up restoration are not particularly great. Also, note how rust has got hold of this model by the seam and despite Volkswagen's preventative medicine of the mid-1980s, the reputation isn't good.

T4   2
Why? There are plenty of T4s in good condition to purchase. If you do restore one, you won't get your money back.

T5   0
No!

→ Finding unroadworthy garage projects to photograph isn't that easy, but here's a T3 that has been stored for a good number of years. Would you restore this – probably questionable.

CHAPTER 3
CONCERNING MATTERS
BUDGETARY

After considerable thought, it was decided to offer real monetary values for the five generations of VW Campers, rather than evolve a complicated rating system, which could well leave accuracy to the imagination. Here then is a snapshot of prices as they stood at the point the fifth-generation Transporter was about to make way in Volkswagen's showrooms for the sixth. Realistically, the only victim of this change is likely to be the T5, already inevitably subject to levels of depreciation associated with any new, or nearly new, car or commercial. For a time at least, prices are likely to tumble a little faster as the affluent with a great desire to keep up with the Joneses steer away from yesterday's model.

➜ Going up! A decent T3 commands more money than it did a decade ago. A bad one a decade ago probably won't exist today.

SUMMARISING VALUES

For many years now, the prices of first-generation VW Campers have continued to spiral upwards. The more difficult times experienced by most in Britain and beyond in recent years seem to have had little if any effect on prices. Indeed, there are those who would argue that low interest rates and difficulties associated with making an honest crust out of money have encouraged more to put their hard-earned into something that will genuinely appreciate and give them a great deal of enjoyment at the same time. It is probable that first-generation prices won't continue to escalate at the same rate they did even as recently as the onset of recession. However, it is equally likely that values won't drop either – the law of ever more difficult rust-free supply and ongoing fever-pitch demand (that shows no sign of declining) dictates that too.

As good first-generation Campers climbed beyond the reach of many, inevitably the prices asked for the next best thing, the second-generation Transporter, became ever firmer. Indeed, it is fair to say that in more recent years, including those of a recessionary nature, prices for genuinely good second-generation VW Campers have escalated more (at least in percentage terms) than values for the first. The gap is

⬇ Going down! A T4 cannot be described as an investment, but depreciation is now minimal in most cases.

still there – after all the cost of an exceptional first-generation Camper is truly mind-boggling nowadays – but it is narrower than it was and the most likely prediction is that this trend will continue. Conversely, whereas the purchase of a first-generation Transporter in well-worn to ominous, or even decidedly bad condition will be likely to cost a sum open to ridicule by those not in the know, there is still a sufficiency of second-generation VW Campers about in these dubious categories to suggest reasonably moderate prices.

However, one thing is as certain as any prophecy can ever be: the second-generation Transporter isn't going to fall by the wayside and only the purchaser who ignores all the guidelines offered elsewhere in this guide, or selects a rust bucket at a grossly inflated asking price, is in serious danger of losing money over the next few years.

Logically, if the price of good first- and second-generation VW Campers is either astronomical or simply costly, demand for a first-class T3 should be on the upward march. To be fair, to a small extent this is correct, but in the UK at least, prices definitely haven't rocketed. By comparison, the US love affair with the Vanagon and Vanagon Camper appears more passionate. Certainly, a quick check on any American based or dominated site would lead the unwary to believe that a decent T3 commanded prices equivalent to many second-generation Transporters. (As the supply of the T4 to the USA was spasmodic and the T5 has been singular in its absence, perhaps there is at least a partial explanation for the Vanagon's American fan club.) To reaffirm, in the UK the story is of gentle increases in prices over the years for decent air-cooled T3s and equally moderate growth for selected and invariably late water-cooled examples. Garden ornament T3s and rusty-seam models are plentiful, which predictably helps to keep prices low, as does the rather obvious lack of intense demand for top-notch examples.

Naturally, the demand for rust-free T3 imports is suppressed by moderate prices in Britain and firm prices across the pond. As a result of such a multitude of imponderables, it is probably wisest to suggest that a T3 is a reasonably high-risk investment and that a genuine love of this generation should be the only motive for purchase.

Having summarised the potential of the vintage VW Campers built between 1950 and 1990(2), attention is turned to what must be described as their modern-day counterparts. Realistically, neither the T4 nor particularly the T5 can be regarded as an investment. Buy now and sell in three, four, five or even ten years' time and with the T4 you might just possibly get your initial outlay back, providing you haven't opted for a fully fledged Camper conversion produced by one of a series of well-known makers. Here, prices are still sufficiently firm that further

← The second-generation Transporter currently provides the best investment potential of them all as prices are rising (have risen) rapidly and look set to continue. A word of warning though, compare the market and don't buy one at an inflated price.

depreciation is inevitable and particularly so until specialist Camper dealers decide that any T4 is too long in the tooth to stand on their mixed-marque forecourts.

For a number of years to come the T5 will suffer reasonably heady depreciation, with the later models suffering most. Owners of vans ripe for conversion to Campers and home-spun weekenders will experience anguish more than recognised professional conversions, which will be sold at VW Van Centres for a time and more particularly at specialist dealerships for a decade and longer at least, depending on the age of the T5 now.

BUDGETS AND INVESTMENT POTENTIAL – THE FULL STORY

Far from an exact science but as a partial aid to potential value, the rarity or availability of a category of vehicle is included in all price charts covering Campers built before 1990. The categories are: Extremely Rare, Very Rare, Rare, Reasonably Rare, Usually Available and Available.

FIRST-GENERATION CAMPER

As an opener to asking prices for the first-generation Transporter/Camper, below are five genuine, albeit edited, adverts from magazines or websites illustrating both the wide variety of asking prices and the varying nature of the vehicles on offer. The most expensive example found when the above adverts were selected had an asking price of £70,000, while somewhat at the other end of the scale a bare-bones restoration project (with history) topped the scales at £16,000. Interestingly, the shell of an SO42 Westfalia Camper and a collection of parts necessary to trim the vehicle when the restoration had been completed were offered at just £7,900, immediately illustrating that indicating definitive prices is far from easy.

Many years ago now it was possible to purchase a first-generation

⬇ Concours entrant first-generation Camper equates to a big asking price but also an appreciating asset.

THE CONCOURS ENTRANT
1955 – BARN DOOR KOMBI   £50,000

20-year, bare metal restoration project using NOS or original style German parts. Multi award winning concours entrant. Includes: original pressed bumpers, fully overhauled 30PS engine, 'bubble' tail lights Hella original, original reflectors, early brake light engine lid, correct 6-volt electrics, original style interior with correct headlining and upholstery.

⬆ This one is in VW's museum in Wolfsburg, but if it were for sale it would no doubt top any price prediction as it dates from 1951.

⬇ Pre-1958 Micro Bus, worth a fortune and a worthy winner at any concours event.

⬆ A pair of very early Micro Bus De Luxe models – premium prices guaranteed.

A CAMPER TO USE, NOT TO COSSET
1962 – 11 WINDOW WALK-THROUGH CAMPER   £21,000

Sailed through the MoT with no advisories and runs very nicely. 1600cc
engine gives a bit more zip than the 1200cc version fitted at the factory.
Full-width rock 'n' roll bed with matching colour seats and three lap belts.
Resident in the UK throughout – first registered Feb 1962.

⬆ Camping at a show.   ⬇ Lovely view first thing in a morning.   ⬆ A customised Camper to use.

CONCERNING MATTERS BUDGETARY CHAPTER 3

RIPE TO ENHANCE TO ORIGINAL OR CUSTOMISED SPECIFICATION
1964 – RIVIERA CAMPER   £15,000

An original paint 1964 Riviera conversion. Imported from California.
Brakes rebuilt. Vehicle in solid condition. Engine required, seats need
re-trimming and some electrical tasks required. Work necessary can
be done which will result in an asking price of £19,999

⬆ A sound vehicle
worthy of substantial
investment.

⬇ Easy to upgrade
if that's an owner's
desire.

⬇ Probably the owners prefers it
this way but transformation to a
concours Samba would be feasible.

THE CUSTOMISED CAMPER TO PERSONAL TASTE
1965 – 21 WINDOW SAMBA   £40,000

Full restoration in 2010. 1,914cc engine by well-known supplier. Twin IDF
Carbs, Engle 130 Cam, 044 heads. Stainless-steel exhaust. Beetle 1303S
gearbox, new clutch fitted. Front wishbone and steering kit, front disc
brake conversion, new late Bay drums on rear. IRS

⬆ Lightly customised
– chrome bumpers,
side step, lowered
etc. Condition –
first class.

⬅ Booking in at a
custom concours
– lovely paint job.

Transporter for a few hundred Pounds, Dollars or Deutschmarks. At the time, the VW Beetle was more popular and as a result attracted higher prices than the older generations of VW Camper. Essentially, just as now, a brand new VW Camper cost a great deal of money and was recognised by the camping fraternity as one of the best on the market. While it would undoubtedly depreciate in value year on year, its ability to retain reasonable residuals was reassuring to those in the market for a trade-in for a new Camper, or hoping to upgrade to a newer second-hand model. Genuine Volkswagen enthusiasts were few and far between so, for example, in 1980, when the youngest first-generation Transporter was 13 years old and many were over 20, their value had reached rock bottom.

⬆ Customising is invariably most successful when stunning paint catches the passing eye.

Nowadays a tip-top original first-generation Transporter of any age is likely to cost almost as much as, if not more than, a brand new VW Camper straight out of the showroom. Realistically, a 1960s VW Camper of original specification, bespoke interior, or lightly customised exterior and interior will not be far behind. Rust-free imports from the USA, and Australia most notably, are no longer as easy to obtain as they once were and as such the price for these has also escalated. Less-than-pristine VW Campers also attract big

A POTENTIAL INVESTMENT
1960 – AUSTRALIAN IMPORT RESTORATION PROJECT   £9,950
Shell in primer, new front sills, original glass. Floor etc. required.
Brand new 1600 engine included in sale. Original gearbox. RHD

⬆ Very few first-generation Campers aren't worth restoring. This one is going to cost a great deal of money if visible filler and rust is an indication of what lurks beneath.

⬅ Restoration or rat-look, the former might involve a trip to see the bank manager.

FIRST-GENERATION CAMPER – 'BARN-DOOR' (1950–1955)

Pristine original or fully restored example, eminently suitable for concours
From £40,000 upwards – possibly as high as £70,000
Extremely Rare

Restored and customised with bespoke interior, bigger engine and lowered
From £35,000 upwards – possibly as high as £65,000
Extremely Rare

'Lived-in' example, with worn but functional interior, possible traces of bubbling paint, either larger or original engine
From £30,000 upwards – could well see a £45,000 asking price
Very Rare

Awaiting restoration – probably/possibly a non-runner
Probably up to £20,000
Very Rare

⬇ This beautiful Chestnut Brown over Sealing Wax Red 'Barn-Door' Samba should be worth £70,000 of anyone's spare cash.

FIRST-GENERATION CAMPER – 'SMALL WINDOW' (1955–1963)

Pristine original or fully restored example, eminently suitable for concours
Theoretically the older the vehicle the rarer it will be and the greater the value it will command. Find a genuine original Camper, e.g. Westfalia SO23/SO34, Devon Caravette etc., and the value should rocket. 1962 Original Camper – up to £50,000
Very Rare

Restored and customised with bespoke interior, bigger engine and lowered
From £25,000 upwards – possibly topping £45,000
Reasonably Rare

'Lived-in' example, with worn but functional interior, possible traces of bubbling paint, either larger or original engine
From £20,000 upwards – heading well into the £30,000-plus range
Usually Available

Awaiting restoration – probably/possibly a non-runner
How much is there left of it and are there some, or all, of the parts required to complete a restoration? From around £6,000 to £10,000-plus
Usually Available

← Immaculate example from the 1950s. Note how the tyres have been blacked to make the vehicle look even more pristine.

prices and while a solid but tired Camper could be a good investment, the biggest danger is the badly restored vehicle with a high asking price. Unrestored, unmolested first-generation Transporters, shells or otherwise, are growing increasingly scarce but, despite high-ticket prices, can still be worthy of consideration. Heavily customised and most noticeably 'rat-look' Campers (deliberately battered, lowered and apparently rusty vehicles) are probably the most risky to purchase after the base category of badly restored examples.

You will be extremely fortunate to find a genuine bargain first-generation Camper and you will need substantial funds in your bank account. The earlier the model, the less difference it will make whether your purchase is a left- or right-hand-drive vehicle.

FIRST-GENERATION CAMPER – 'LARGE WINDOW' (1963–1967)

Pristine original or fully restored example, eminently suitable for concours
£40,000 as a guide. A fully fledged Camper will attract more bids than a budget model, while, for example, a Kombi, which could be adapted for an occasional overnight, should be less.
Reasonably rare

Restored and customised with bespoke interior, bigger engine and lowered
From £25,000 to £40,000 as a guide. The vehicle has got to be good to hit the upper end of this range, but with customised vehicles it is always at least partly about personal preferences.
Usually Available

'Lived-in' example, with worn but functional interior, possible traces of bubbling paint, either larger or original engine
£15,000 to £25,000 The better it is the higher the price. However, don't pay over the odds in this category as, in terms of choice, there are more here than in any other first-generation category.
Available

Awaiting restoration – probably/possibly a non-runner
£5,000 as a starting point and probably a relatively ropey one. However, please bear in mind that, unless long nights in a cold dreary garage is your thing, or you want to burn a few notes by handing your wreck over to the professionals, there are plentiful options in other categories covering this age range.
Available

SECOND-GENERATION CAMPER

The law of supply and demand dictates that as the first-generation Transporter became increasingly expensive, the value of its successor would increase. This indeed has been the case and for a decent second-generation model nowadays you can expect to have to pay well into the tens of thousands of pounds, although there are a reasonable number of adverts where owners are testing the water and asking several thousand pounds more. Some importers are looking for these kinds of sums too and, as has been suggested, with the flow becoming more restricted, prices of vehicles from 'rust-free' countries will become ever firmer.

Unlike examples of the first-generation Transporter, it would be unfair to distinguish between an early and late model in terms of value, although it might possibly be prudent to suggest that, in terms of original specification Campers, a Westfalia conversion, for example, might be marginally more expensive than some other brands. Bear in mind that the ranks of well-kitted-out Campmobiles invariably seen at shows and gatherings are from the Westfalia stable and tend to be towards the upper echelons in the specification stakes. If solid wood, or even top-quality ply is your preference, then the cost-cutting necessary

⬇ This early second-generation Devon top-of-the-range Eurovette Camper has won many concours awards thanks to its truly stunning originality and the pristine nature of its interior.

THE CONCOURS ENTRANT OR PERFECT ORIGINAL EQUIPMENT CAMPER
1977 – UNRESTORED WESTFALIA BERLIN   £29,000

Two-owner, unrestored Westfalia, original paint, original interior, never welded, just stunning inside and out. No rust issues, never involved in an accident. No dents. Sleeps four adults, has a cooker, fridge, stove, original table and buddy seat. Fitted with original Philips Radio, original 'thermo glas' and an original Westfalia tow hitch.

← This late model second-generation Camper has a novelty aspect to it that shouldn't affect a concours judge's judgement. It is a special model built to celebrate Devon's 21st anniversary.

→ Resident in Volkswagen's museum in Wolfsburg, this Camper is in wonderful original condition and would be likely to win any concours entered by the company.

A CAMPER TO USE, NOT TO COSSET
1971 – DORMOBILE   £13,500

Early Bay, tax exempt, full MoT. Original Dormobile interior, including rock
'n roll bed, 2 hammocks, cooker, cool-box, sink etc., lovely condition, drives
very well, exterior respray, custom wheels and looks stunning.

↑ → More practical
than a first-generation
model, slightly more
powerful and full of
retro appeal.

There are so many much-loved Campers in this category. Most are polished to perfection, sport the odd accessory and might well have been repainted.

as recession hit in the mid 1970s will prompt you to buy an earlier, rather than later second-generation model. Also note that by the end of the decade the dreaded word 'chipboard' was beginning to raise its ugly head.

Likewise, original budget conversions, deliberately intended for casual stopovers, rather than full Campers, cushioned with all the amenities afforded in the 1970s, will tend to be offered with lower price labels as they don't meet modern criteria. (Take a look at the potted model guide to Devon Conversions of this era.) Of course, a particularly pristine example might be the exception to the rule and, should the opportunity arise to bag a bargain, the entrepreneur could well look at a profitable resale and, as a result, the equivalent of 'money off' what was his or her original intended purchase.

Perhaps too, the seller might up the price a little if the vehicle is possessed of one of Volkswagen's larger engines. Okay, they are thirsty but realistically so is the great survivor, the 1,584cc 1600. With the 1.7-, 1.8- and particularly the 2.0-litre engines, at least the opportunity might arise to overtake a slow-moving vehicle ... possibly even a second-generation Transporter powered by the 1600 engine!

Second-generation Transporters lend themselves just as well as their predecessor to bespoke interiors and highly attractive, if non-

⬇ Non-standard colour combination, black bumpers and VW roundel, clear indicator lenses, 'fancy' wheels and foot rail – all fairly standard in the world of customising and in this instance, very tastefully accomplished.

LIGHTLY CUSTOMISED CAMPER FOR WEEKENDS AND HOLIDAYS
1969 – VW CAMPER   £11,500

Original UK Bus, Tax & MoT. Recent interior refurb. Full Camping unit
with Double Cooker, ¾ rock 'n' roll bed. Red seats with Cream piping.
New headlining. Flip-down TV/DVD player. Red/white flooring and
carpet set. 240v hook-up, 12v leisure battery. Extras include roof rack,
side step, jail-bars, Empi alloy wheels. 1600cc engine.

↑ ➜ The lightly
customised second-
generation Camper
is just as popular and
loved as the more
original offering.
Prices checked
suggest they are
slightly cheaper to
buy, but there are
always exceptions
to the rule.

THE CUSTOMISED CAMPER TO PERSONAL TASTE
1967 – ONE YEAR CALIFORNIA IMPORT – WESTFALIA PATINA £12,000

1600tp twin-carb 75amp alternator, split charge, twin batteries, Petronix ignition,
electric fuel pump, Empi quiet-pack. ¾ rock 'n' roll bed, Kustom Inertia cabinets, wardrobe
and dicky seat. Twin ring and grill/cool-box, Propex heater, inverter, Newton Commercial
front seats with matching panels. Front: Creative 4in narrowed beam, French slammer,
dropped spindles, late Bay discs. Rear: Creative 2in dropped adjustable spring plates,
Spax adjustable shocks. Runs nice and low. Bodywork is solid but carries history.

← 'Rat-look' second-
generation Transporter –
how do you place a value
on this kind of vehicle?

↓ Heavily customised
second-generation
Campers aren't abundant
in number. Look at the
orange vehicle ... yes,
it's a Bay masquerading
as a Split. That's heavy
customising.

A POTENTIAL INVESTMENT
1974 – DEVON CAMPER   £4,500

An ideal project for the enthusiast. Original Devon interior in good condition
with rock 'n' roll bed, cooker, sink, cool-box and hammocks in pop-top.
Needs work on the underside and has patches of rust on the bodywork.

⬆ ➡ This rather
battered pair of early
second-generation
Campers exhibit
potential despite the
dented body panels and
flat or even assorted
paintwork. Both have
elevating roofs and
neither show outward
evidence of the
more costly signs of
potentially terminal rot.

SECOND-GENERATION CAMPER
RECOGNISED ORIGINAL-SPEC CAMPER CONVERSIONS

Pristine original or fully restored example, eminently suitable for concours
£29,000 as in the advert on page 75 is an awful lot of money and the vehicle must have
been really special to tempt even the most frivolous purchaser. Realistically, you should
be able to pick up a vehicle qualifying for this category for £20,000 – possibly slightly less
although increasingly, slightly more.
Reasonably Rare

**'Lived-in' example, with worn but functional interior, possible traces of bubbling
paint, either larger or original engine**
Shall we say £11,000 to £14,000 and for the latter there must not be a bubble in sight. Most
second-generation models seen clustered in friendly camping groups or clubs fall into this
category. Not perfect – after all none are spring chickens – but all are loved.
Readily Available

Awaiting restoration – probably/possibly a non-runner
As rust-free examples from sun-soaked States such as California, or possibly Australia,
become much more scarce than they once were, shells and wrecks creep up in price. No
interior, or a wrecked one and the prices tumble in this category. Rotten body and it might
be best to search again. £2,000 to £5,000
Available

➜ Here's a typical
crossover second-
generation model.
While this vehicle is a
welcome participant in
a club display, its owner
probably wouldn't
dream of entering a
concours class. To
describe it as simply
'lived in' is a bit of an
insult and explains why
values in such a class
vary tremendously. This
vehicle has to be worth
at least £20,000.

SECOND-GENERATION CAMPER
A CAMPER WHERE ORIGINALITY COUNTS FOR LITTLE

Restored and customised with bespoke interior, bigger engine and lowered
Custom concours territory possibly, or a refurbishment that brings a great deal of pleasure to owners. Only one downside: it's bespoke so might not sell as easily as you think it should, simply because personal taste varies so much. How about a valuation of £12,000 to £20,000 top-notch. It's vague, but so is the marketplace.
Usually Available

'Lived-in' example, with worn but functional interior, possible traces of bubbling paint, either larger or original engine
Definitely not concours, but otherwise similar to 'restored and customised' but not as good. Either more noticeably DIY, or condition a notch down. Yes to the odd bubble and a nod too to the 'lived-in' look. Good at £10,000, even better if you spot a decent one for less, but probably worth having another look if the price is creeping much into five figures.
Readily Available

Awaiting restoration – probably/possibly a non-runner
Buy a shell and if you are good at welding, designing and creating an interior, you could be quids in. The better the body, the more it will cost. Don't pay for an interior you intend to rip out. Maximum £3,000 but try for less, much less.
Available

original, exterior work. It will be possible to buy such a VW Camper 'off the shelf' as it were, but bear in mind that just like buying a house, some features might not to be your liking and there will be additional costs to rectify matters. Similarly, with an eye on your second-generation bespoke Camper as an investment, it is conceivable that if you sell, the purchaser will have similar thoughts and bargain with you to cover his or her planned expenditure.

A solid Transporter, or one requiring light restoration, might well be the kind of vehicle to look at if the plan is to create a second-generation Camper to your own colour scheme and interior design layout. What will be obvious is that you will be unfortunate if you lose money if you come to sell it in years to come. The second-generation Camper is possibly the soundest investment of all. Prices have risen for a number of years and the prediction has to be that they will continue to climb out of proportion to general trends.

Before turning to the next generation of VW Camper it is worth

mentioning once more the second-generation Transporter produced in Brazil until 2013. On the plus side, they are all newish, or at least are likely to have been manufactured some 20 years or more after the demise of their German counterparts. From November 2005, such Transporters were powered by a 1,390cc water-cooled engine purloined from a passing VW Polo or Fox. Listing the negatives, probably the biggest is the Brazilian climate and hence the attendant lack of factory-applied protection against rust. Newness also implies depreciation and the combination of the two might incline some to steer clear.

Having said all that, a trawl of the Danbury Conversions website at the point this book was being written, followed by a delve into the ethereal columns of AutoTrader, not only revealed the supremely luxurious 2009 model detailed opposite, but a wealth of other price information guaranteed to warm the cockles of a current owner. Here are a few examples, all of which displayed the trappings of a truly de luxe internal specification: Unused models, 2013 spec, from £33,849 (trade); 2013, 9,421 miles on the clock, £39,995 (trade); 2007, 26,000 miles, £25,995 (private sale); 2005, 60,000 miles, £22,995 (trade).

2009 – VOLKSWAGEN DANBURY DIAMOND BRAZILIAN CAMPERVAN IN ORANGE AND WHITE, 13,000 MILES

Taxed, full service history and two sets of keys. Danbury documentation. Water-cooled 1,390cc petrol and bi-fuel. Full leather interior, Cream with burnt orange piping. Centre console with matching leather armrest. Buddy seat with matching leather seat. Interior spare wheel cover in matching leather. Wood laminate finish to centre floor area. Top quality Wilton carpets in beige to front cabin and centre floor area. Finished with leather bindings. Centre area carpet has colour coded storage bag. Front cabin has removable over carpets, finished in beige with leather bindings, again in top quality Wilton. All interior curtains, two round armrest cushions, upper roof double bed mattress cover and tablecloth, all matching design colour, curtains have magnets concealed in them for privacy adjustment. Blackout blinds and rear door mosquito net. Pop-up roof with tinted sunroof. King size rock 'n' roll bed. Front and rear heating. Two burner gas hob and grill, dual fridge. Removable table. Tinted privacy glass. Lowered suspension, alloy wheels (including spare) with VW centres and matching VW valve cap tops. Low profile tyres (including spare). Power steering. Front and rear three-point anchored seat belts. Front roof rack. Aluminium side step. Parking sensors. Reverse Camera. Flat-screen TV – flip-down with digital Freeview and DVD. CD, iPod/Pad, Playstation aux connection. Flip-up Alpine touch-screen television with sat nav, Bluetooth in dash. £42,000

THIRD-GENERATION CAMPER

It should follow that if the second-generation Transporter is becoming more expensive then prices of its successor will also start to creep up, and to some extent this is true. However, the T3 lacks the retro charm of its predecessors and, to some minds at least, is blighted by out-of-favour 1980s design.

For those diehards for whom any form of cooling other than traditional air is sacrilege, the third-generation Camper is only acceptable in the early years of its production. The 1600 air-cooled engine is definitely underpowered, more so than it ever was in the T3's predecessor, and realistically, although costing more, in terms of contentment a second-generation Camper, wrapped in its comfort blanket of traditionalism, is a much better proposition ... until prices rise to current first-generation levels.

↑ → There aren't that many classic concours T3 models about. This one has had one owner from new and has been used as Hanover intended as well as winning rosettes. Difficult to price – the model isn't the most popular, but the condition is superb. On a good day with an eager buyer, £15,000?

THIRD-GENERATION CAMPERS FOR SALE

A cross-section of recently written adverts illustrating owners' expectations when offering their vehicles for sale:

1984 – T3 WESTFALIA JOKER   £10,000
Nice original LHD yellow T3, 1600 diesel engine, only three owners from new. Full service history. Drives and runs okay. All typical weak spots of the T3 are okay. Sleeps two, has a fridge, pilot seats, cooker, sink, tow hitch etc.
Potential concours entrant, or lovely original equipment Camper

1989 – WESTFALIA CALIFORNIA   £9,000
LHD German import. 1600 turbo diesel, lots of history, fantastic condition, all mod cons – fridge, cooker, 240v, pop-top. Taxed and tested. Will be hard to find better.
A top-notch Camper to use, not to cosset

1982 – AIR-COOLED KARMANN GYPSY   £9,500
LHD, 2.0 litre, 65,000kms from new on unmodified Type 4 engine. 4-speed manual gearbox. Original paint, very tidy and original inside and out. Spec includes shower room, large double bed, seating area at the rear and sleeping for two children over cab. Passenger seat swivels.
A Camper designed to offer more room and more facilities

1981 – T3 AIR-COOLED 'TWIN-SLIDER'   £6,000
Rare twin-slider in VW Bamboo Yellow and Ivory. Bodywork, paint in excellent condition with only a couple of minor imperfections, rare to find with complete interior. 2.0 CU Type 4 twin carbs, lowered suspension H+R springs, Koni shocks – rides low and firm, 17in Porsche Cub wheels, Bugpack quiet pack, LA Performance 3 Tubes, rear jail-bars, Westfalia tow bar.
The customised Camper to personal taste

1984 – T3 CAMPER   £3,999
65,000 miles on new engine 1.6D. Porsche wheels – 18in 265x35 rear, 225x18 front. Correct ET 35, fully fitted out interior with carpet and all fittings, all clean and tidy. Full berth fold bed with cushions. Been very reliable. Year's MoT.
Homespun Camper interior, lightly modified external appearance.

↑ This Holdsworth Camper provides a typical example of a vehicle intended for use at weekends and during holiday periods. Like the examples on the page opposite, it is likely to command a value of less than £10,000, a sum that may increase and certainly won't fall, providing its current condition is maintained.

Correspondingly, for those who couldn't care less about the pureness of air-cooled motoring, when it comes to the choice between a petrol-engined T3 or a T4, delving a little deeper into the pocket for the latter shouldn't really be a difficult decision. Pedestrian diesel performance in the T3 era should make the decision to upgrade to a more powerful and genuinely fuel-efficient T4 even easier.

Having generally battered and bruised the prospects of the T3 owner wishing to sell his or her Camper, it should be quickly stated that a late model, original specification vehicle will exhibit a degree of sophistication unheard of in any German-manufactured second-generation model. Campers such as Westfalia's California and Atlantic, Autohomes' Kamper, Holdsworth's Villa 3 et al, are spacious, inviting and, with others, generally benefit from big advances in the design of elevating and fixed high roofs. These models and an original specification, early 2.0-litre air-cooled model are appreciating and are likely to continue so to do.

Whether you could expect to sell a bespoke interior model at a profit, taking into account the costs involved in creating such a specification, is questionable. Of course, you may opt to buy a decent shell, create the interior and exterior looks that you want and keep the vehicle for the foreseeable future. If that is your chosen course

A collection of Campers to use rather than cosset, although each one shows signs that successive owners have lavished care and attention on them resulting in no telltale signs of seam rust. Clockwise from the top of the page: water-cooled Devon, Westfalia Atlantic, slightly updated late-model Devon, Westfalia Joker – each fall into the under £10,000 category.

← Slightly modified, and why not, this Westfalia California is typical of a late-model T3 Camper. Although it is easy to be critical of early 1980s fads and fashions, the same cannot be said of the attractive laminates attributed to the California. Similarly, the equipment level is high. All this for under £10,000 has to be worthy of consideration.

⬇ Designed for two rather than a family, the Holdsworth Vision is a well-appointed conversion available at a reasonable price.

of action, you will definitely be able to undercut the costs of a similar venture with a second-generation Transporter (and by default, a first-generation model).

For the moment, tackling a battered and bruised T3 should not be necessary. There are enough examples about to make avoiding such a move easy. Also, beware the particular breed of tin worm unique to the T3 – the 'seam-burrower'. In an attempt to improve rust protection, Volkswagen filled the T3's body seams with filler. With advancing years, this can dry, crack and fall out, creating an ideal nesting place for the seam-burrower. At all costs, avoid a T3 that exhibits signs of seam rust – possibly the least sound investment across all types of Transporter.

A couple more paragraphs should suffice in the telling of the tale of the third-generation Transporter. First up are the Vanagon and the Vanagon Camper, the USA versions of the T3. In the unlikely event that you ponder the purchase of a rust-free example from the other side of the pond, be aware that the average American's love affair with such models appears to be stronger, some might even say much stronger, than ours in the UK and those of mainland Europe.

⬆ This air-cooled Danbury conversion had been given a very professional new coat of paint when it was photographed. While there was no evidence in this instance of disguising a multitude of sins and the vehicle wasn't for sale, beware the seller who has organised a quick respray immediately before you visit!

↑ A near-perfect
Multivan, LHD of
course. Lovely
weekenders, and still
about for under the
magic sum of £10,000.

➜ Karmann's Gipsy
and Cheetah add a
different dimension
to T3 ownership at
a budget price.

As a result, the gap in dollar prices between a second-generation
model and a Vanagon is less and we could argue that US vehicles
are overpriced. The spec is high as might be anticipated but so is the
asking price. The probable answer is to stay away, or, of course, buy
one already imported and therefore subject to market demand here,
at the appropriate price.

Without doubt, the syncro models (that's the ones with a form of
permanent four-wheel-drive) have a following, although the number
of Campers in this form are relatively few, the preference seemingly
being for the camping-shy Double Cab Pick-up. Let's say that if your
path crosses with that of a genuine syncro Camper (either converted
by a recognised manufacturer at the time, or of a bespoke home-
spun nature, expect to pay more than anything suggested in the T3
category chart on page 95. Also, take note that it is possible to own
a T3 syncro that is newer than an early T4. That's because the four-
wheel-drive T3 continued to be produced for two years after the T4
was launched. Some of the late models are rather tasty too. What is
it about a VW that warms you to a model and a generation that you
have been determined to criticise!

← ↑ Expendable runabouts for well under £5,000, just for the fun of it, but how long will these Campers last without expensive restoration work?

THIRD-GENERATION CAMPER

Top-notch original, or carefully refurbished example of a Camper from a recognised manufacturer
A few really stunning original examples exist and occasionally, as in one of the adverts on page 87, such a T3 is offered for sale. A top-notch Camper does a great deal to restore your faith in the third-generation. If it's a restored one, take care to check out a newly painted example, just in case there's seam rot just waiting to bubble out again. £10,000 is a lot of money for a T3, so the Camper must be exceptional. Hopefully, you'll clinch a deal at £8,000 or less, but the rarity of the model in this kind of condition helps to inflate the price.
Reasonably Rare*

Restored and customised with bespoke interior, alloys and slightly lowered
Finding a really good T3 of this type isn't going to be that easy. More are likely to portray odd signs of wear and tear, either internally or externally. The usual rules apply, at least as far as lowering etc. Make sure it's fit for purpose. Up to £9,000 if it's a really good one, but you could expect to find one of these for considerably less.
Reasonably Rare**

'Lived-in' example, with worn but functional interior, possible traces of bubbling paint, the odd seam issue, and its original engine
This is what you see out and about at the favourite watering holes of the average VW enthusiast, be it at a show or beside the seaside. Ideal for would-be owners either who can't afford an earlier generation model, or who simply begrudge spending money. It's certainly a way of being involved on a budget, but like many economy buys, it might not last all that long, or cost a packet of unredeemable cash to keep it on the road. £2,500, possibly less, up to £4,000 maximum (but always try to negotiate).
Available

Camper Awaiting restoration – probably/possibly a non-runner
If the vehicle has lost the majority of its interior or it's decidedly shabby, only a good body would redeem it. However, body rot should be avoided at all costs. Why buy such a vehicle? Max £1,000.
Available

* The logic of the rating 'Reasonably Rare' in the case of an original T3 is not one of demand but realistically due to the ravages of the tin worm.
** 'Reasonably Rare' with regard to a customised T3 is related to the comparative lack of interest in the generation and the preference of many of those who opt to customise a vehicle from an earlier, or possibly later, generation of Camper.

FOURTH-GENERATION CAMPER

Working on the principle that more owners of a T4 Camper will simply want to use the vehicle for weekends and holidays, rather than become wrapped up in the VW enthusiast scene, three of the examples opposite might well prove ideal for such purposes. Note, however, that the newer the vehicle and the fewer the miles on the clock, the more the purchaser will have to pay. As an example, a 2003 Auto-Sleeper Clubman 2.5TDI with just 22,500 miles on the clock commanded a price of £23,995, while a not dissimilar model, a Gatcombe of 2001 vintage with a recorded mileage of 37,000 miles attracted a hefty £22,995 in 2015.

For the moment at least, the T4 has a dual status when it comes to values. Theoretically, a vehicle that was superseded as long ago as 2003 should have completed its downward spiral as far as depreciation goes and this is probably true in the instance of nearly all early models. However, if the T4 you are looking at is a fully authenticated Camper, worthy of inclusion on the forecourt of either a specialist dealer, or conceivably more general second-hand car lots, this might not

⬇ This late model, long-nose Bilbo's Celeste has carried off concours prizes but also travelled all over Europe. Depreciation is still about, but in 2015 one could expect to pay over £20,000 for a vehicle of this quality.

FOURTH-GENERATION CAMPERS FOR SALE

2001 VW T4 AUTO-SLEEPER, TRIDENT   £18,995
59,900 miles, 2.5TDI diesel, automatic. Five owners. CD player, tow bar,
2+2 berth, rear belts, heating, leisure battery, mains, fridge freezer, grill,
hob, side kitchen, sink drainer, double bed, wardrobe, awning, blinds,
carpets, curtains, fly-screens, on-board water tank, power steering.
Won't be here long.
A Camper to use. Recognised conversion

1993 VW T4 AUTO-SLEEPER, CLUBMAN   £12,995
Automatic, 2.4 Diesel, power steering, Only 70,000 miles. Auto-Sleeper
monocoque body. Superb build quality. Rear corner washroom with
cassette toilet and shower. Rear kitchen with oven, grill and hobs. 3-way
fridge, sink and drainer. Loads of storage throughout. 2 single beds or one
large double. Double-glazed windows with fly nets and blackout blinds.
Heating and hot water. Large wind out awning etc.
A Camper to use. Recognised conversion

1997 VW T4 REIMO, LUCKY   £9,995
2.5TDI. Rock 'n' roll bed plus roof bed, fridge 2-burner stove plus grill,
sink and water tank. Zig leisure battery and Battery Mate. Rear seat belts.
Full service history, belts done at 68K. 85K with MoTs to confirm. Only
two previous keepers.
A Camper to use. Recognised conversion

1994 T4 TRANSPORTER CAMPER VAN   £5,995
Full respray along with four arch panels. Full Camper conversion on
carbon-fibre furniture. Split charge. Smev sink and hob. Rock 'n' roll bed.
12/240v. Black and red leatherette seats and mattress. Excellent condition.
*A bespoke conversion offering an interior suited to the tastes of
the installer*

2001 T4 DELIVERY VAN   £5,750
Fantastic T4 in white with cool monster logos around body. Full MoT,
FSH. Low miles 105k. 18in alloys, ply-lined and carpeted in rear. PAS,
stereo. Ideal for full Camper conversion.
A vehicle ripe for bespoke Camper conversion

← While our 'concours' example of a T4 has a traditional elevating roof, a great number of T4 conversions feature high fixed tops. The Autohomes Komet (bottom) is traditional in that it is based on a SWB T4, but the two Californias (both LHD of course) make use of the LWB T4. Condition is everything, but all the examples pictured would carry a reasonable price tag if offered for sale.

necessarily be the case. So long as the T5 can be purchased brand new from Volkswagen, its predecessor, at least in Camper guise, has credence. Now, with the arrival of the sixth-generation Transporter, the T5 adopts the credentials of the T4. Surely, the time can't be that far off when a T4 is banished to the sales territories frequented by earlier generations.

⬆ The roomy Compass Navigator.

One further complication arises. The T4 is incredibly popular as a vehicle for customising (as are earlier and no doubt later examples of the T5). Assuming the work done on what might once have been a Delivery Van (or a basic form of windowed vehicle) includes its transformation into a Camper, which most projects encompass, then forget the rule that the vehicle may well have reached rock bottom. Bearing in mind the relative lack of interest in the T3 and the combination of an attractive body shape and relatively modern engines, this type of T4 might well be appreciating, albeit gently.

A pristine, low mileage for its year, fully fledged 'authentic' Camper is the vehicle most likely to vary widely in the seller's asking price. It is likely that a dealer (and make no mistake, trade if not brand dealers are still interested in the T4) will be asking more than a private seller, as will a long-term owner who can provide a full service history.

↑ Auto-Sleepers: masters of the big body mounted on the T4 chassis platform. Quietly depreciating, but in 2015 still worth over £20,000.

Also, as the conversion companies could select between short- and long-wheelbase models for the first time, or even more significantly could develop a full body to lower gently behind the chassis cab, premiums can be anticipated for bigger vehicles. Without doubt, an Auto-Sleeper (for example) with a purpose-designed fibreglass living compartment is a thing of spacious beauty (at least compared to the cramped living quarters and basic equipment of earlier models.) Shower facilities, an on-board loo and genuinely comfortable dining, seating and sleeping facilities offered in a package near enough to contemporary design to be perfectly acceptable, make the original-spec T4 Camper conversion an attractive proposition.

Possibly, of all the generations, the T4 is currently the most apt to chose for a full, no expense spared, bespoke/customised exterior/interior conversion (providing mercenary investment is not the name of your game). It is certainly going to be a close tie with the second-generation model, but the necessary starter pack for both upgrades, a shell, will cost more and no doubt require more attention in the case of the older Transporter. A cheap serviceable shell makes sense – think rust-free Delivery Van, or budget price 'window van' – with a body of an age that still has a semblance of modernity. While some would regard painting a second-generation Transporter in pearlescent hues as irreverent, few

FOURTH-GENERATION CAMPER

Pristine original Coachbuilt motorhome

To be abundantly clear, here we are talking about a purpose-built body constructed on the T4 chassis platform. Examples include most of the Auto-Sleepers range, Compass models and Auto Trail products. This is luxury VW Camping with more room and invariably more gadgets appropriate to four-star accommodation. Prices will vary considerably between dealers and private sales and to a certain extent will depend as well on the age of the vehicle. If it's affordable, go for a long-nose 2.5TDI, but expect to be parting with a figure well into the tens of thousands of pounds and possibly over £20,000. Lower mileages are always welcome, but the 2.5TDI is good for a couple of times around the clock.

Pristine original Camper – High roof or elevating roof

Essentially, what you are buying here is an updated version of the tried and tested format applied to earlier generations of Campers. The equipment level is likely to be more sophisticated but sadly, the materials used in the conversion will be less robust. Like the motorhome, try for the 2.5TDI. A couple of years ago a concours example was up for sale for a figure in excess of £22,000, but realistically this kind of T4 Camper should cost less than the motorhome variety. You will see examples offered at under £10,000 while others could easily be £15,000 or more. (As per the motorhome, the longer you are reading this book after its publication date, the more the chance depreciation will have played its part.)

'Customised' Camper

If pricing a T4 motorhome or Camper isn't an exact science then suggesting how much you might have to part with for a customised model is about as reliable as predicting the British weather! What can be said is that the 'genuine' dealer is unlikely to have a customised model on his forecourt, which should suggest immediately that the vehicle will be cheaper than its 'standard' counterpart. At £6,000 the example included on page 97 might be a bargain, but there again, without a test drive and personal viewing, it could also be a bodged job worth far less and hence a vehicle to avoid.

Delivery Van or basic window van, ripe for conversion into a customised Camper

A few years ago now, the AA decided to sell off its fleet of T4 breakdown vans. Invariably the bodywork was sound and if it had had a knock then professional repairs had been carried out. Likewise, although the mileage might be on the high side, mechanically, as you would expect of the AA, the vehicles were in tip-top condition. If you are going to create a Camper out of a Delivery Van, or a basic window option, this is the kind of vehicle you should be looking for. Of course, you might opt for a long-nose Caravelle complete with either the 2.5TDI engine or even the VR6/V6 petrol engine. The example on page 97 is not cheap and you should be able to find one for less – considerably less. Try for £2,000!

This is the rarely seen and truly massive Winnebago Rialta. Its overall length extends to 6,299mm.

if any would suggest a non-standard shade, be it from the Volkswagen paint palette or from that of another manufacturer, blasphemy in the case of the T4. Lowering, meaty accessories, super wheels, sonic sound barrier breaking music systems and sumptuous interiors are not going to result in excommunication from the VW fold.

Realistically, it shouldn't take that long to find a workhorse T4 at the price you would be willing to pay for a decent fortnight's holiday for a family of four. Your enthusiasm and passion for the project will ultimately determine the budget and subsequent revisions to create your bespoke Camper and personal statement.

THE T4 MULTIVAN

Do you want a comparatively cheap, totally authentic Camper with the advantages of the 2.5TDI engine, a layout installed from new that doubles as weekend accommodation and daily passenger ferrying? Then opt for Volkswagen's Multivan!

Although the concept given the name of Multivan was devised and road-tested in the days of the T3, the cross between a Camper and a Micro-Bus-style passenger carrier only came into its own during the lifetime of the T4. Lucky souls living in Germany and a good number of other European countries were offered the Multivan, a vehicle with a pull-out bed, collapsible dining table and in some instances facilities to keep food fresh, virtually from day one. In Great Britain surfers, cyclists and others who wanted a base that was more than a van, more than a car, but not a fully fledged Camper had to wait until the arrival of the long-nose T4.

THE T4 MULTIVAN – A SELECTION OF RECENTLY PUBLISHED ADVERTS

VW T4 MULTIVAN 1998 2.5TDI   £7,450

Left hand drive VW Multivan imported from Germany. Usual extras for this
model like pull-out, full-width bed, folding table, six seats (two captain's seats
at the front, one folding captain seat in the back and three-seater pullout bed).
12v power sockets at the back, cup holders, Eberspächer night heater, electric
windows, mirrors and sunroof. The interior is in very good condition with minimal
wear. Starts and drives very well, with no smoke, rattles or any funny noises.

VW T4 MULTIVAN 1998 2.5TDI   £5,400

134,000 miles. First registered 01 08 1998. This is an original Multivan. I believe
that only about 700 were imported to the UK and this must be one of the few
remaining in standard form. It has not been chipped, lowered, or modified in
any way. What has been added (from new) are the following: Reimo roof, awning
rail, tinted windows, roof rack, tow bar, bike rack. It also has the original VW
curtains in excellent order, VW rubber over-mats. This is not a mint-condition
show van but it could easily be. Paintwork mostly original and damage-free.
Some stone chips on the bonnet, but they are small and not obvious. Interior,
no tears and minimal wear. Small fabric snag on driver's seat.

VW T4 MULTIVAN 1999. RARE RHD   £7,995

124,000 miles, two previous owners. Genuine RHD Multivan T4 – rare van in
Surf Blue, lovely drive and condition. 2.5TDI, electric front windows and sliding
rear window. Air conditioning, front airbags, door pockets and rear cup holders.
Side elevating SpaceRoof installed allowing for additional fold-back 2 berths up
top and 8-foot high roof for full van length, with 2 windows and 2 zip-able fly-screens.
7 manufacturer's belted seats, two of which have storage behind and are removable
allowing for extra space or a camping pod to be installed. Rear bench seat folds into
a full width bed. All rear seats can be removed to allow entire load space to be utilised.
Radio cassette, central locking, fold-out table that stores in the side panel.

VW T4 MULTIVAN 2003 2.5TDI   £9,000

Genuine factory-built T4 Multivan. Built in September 2002, first registered in
January 2003. Red. Two non-smoking, non pet owners from new including
myself. Comes with two keys with remotes plus original master key. Some of the
main features include sunroof, air con, tow bar, electric windows, electric mirrors,
convertible double bed, original curtains, fold-out table and Toad security system.
Genuine 84,000 miles. This is a very nice unmodified Multivan best judged with
your own eyes.

FIFTH-GENERATION CAMPER

With the sixth-generation VW Camper about to make its debut, the T5 was relatively straightforward. You can buy the California SE and the California Beach brand, sparkling new from your local Volkswagen Commercial Vehicle Centre, or opt for a new VW Camper courtesy of the many conversion companies that specialise in or include the Volkswagen Transporter in their ranges. Now, of course, the emphasis will shift to the T6, but at least for a number of years, examples of the T5 will be available second-hand at official dealers and for some considerable time at specialist dealers.

⬇ Leading the way, Volkswagen's own Camper, the VW California. Volkswagen's Press Office produced some remarkable imagery guaranteed to make you want to rush out and buy one, while also being handy to celebrate production of the 50,000th California in July 2014.

The big question, however, will be price. Turning back to the T4, while depreciation has been considerable, official conversions are still on offer at significant money. The probability is that the last of the T5s will take a tumble just as any new vehicle does once it is registered and on the road, but the fall will be accentuated by the change of generation back at the VW factory in Hanover.

That being said, earlier models have already experienced modern vehicle depreciation and as the popularity of the T5 is renowned (and

BRAND NEW CAMPERS IN THE FINAL YEAR OF PRODUCTION

Volkswagen's T5 California
- California Beach from
  £36,238

- California SE from
  £45,792

**Auto-Sleepers Group,
Willersey, Worcestershire**
- Topaz 2 berth – turbo diesel 140PS
  Euro V Engine, 2 berth with GRP roof
  high-top, including side windows
  £56,795

- Topaz 2 berth as above, but
  with DSG 'automatic'
  £58,495

Danbury Motor Caravans, Bristol
- Surf (4 or 5 seat layout, low profile
  or high-top roof, based on T5 swb,
  large open living space)
  From £34,249

- Active (high-top or low raising roof,
  several engine options, twin or
  double beds, fixed cassette toilet)
  From £34,249

- Royale (top-of-the-range T5, twin
  or double beds, rear bathroom,
  long wheelbase)
  From £37,999

- Trail (new and used conversions, three
  person rear bench seat, 12-volt power
  socket, sink and fridge freezer)
  From £34,249

Hillside Leisure UK Ltd, Derby
- Thulston Long wheelbase, high-top
  From £40,995

- Cromford Long wheelbase, choice
  of elevating roof or factory high-top
  From £40,995

- Doverage 2 or 4 berth Camper built
  on a short-wheelbase Transporter
  From £37,995

- Buxton long wheelbase conversion
  with specially designed, thermally
  insulated high-top roof
  From £45,595

- Birchover, elevating roof,
  short wheelbase
  £39,995

- Birchover, elevating roof,
  long wheelbase
  £46,099

- Birchover, high-top
  £42,640

Prices of second-hand examples
of the T5 are very firm in the year the
T6 is launched.

unlikely to alter) it seems probable that prices will at least maintain the equilibrium already established. In other words, if the intention is to camp in a window van, or convert a Delivery Van for such a purpose, the financial risk will be no greater than if you had signed a cheque for a similar T4.

To offer guidance on prices and values, various categories of T5 are presented, starting opposite with the RRPs for brand new Campers in the final year of production.

Listed on page 110 are examples of adverts extracted from enthusiast magazines and suitably edited to present generic text. Each represents a different year in the early chronology of the T5 and all are vehicles offered by private sale, having first been converted from either a window van or a Delivery Van at home.

Finally, five examples of pre-face lift vans are listed on page 111, all of which remain as Volkswagen designated them when they were brand new. In all probability, both categories will be subject to ongoing depreciation, while neither will be boosted in value by specialist dealers due to their non-Camper or homebuilt status.

⬇ Finding somewhere to buy a T5 won't be difficult – remember depreciation though!

A host of smaller companies have carried out on conversions on the T5, others have thought of ingenious add-ons, while some owners like to add a little in the way of personalisation, be it extra metalwork, mouldings, shiny bits or effective, distinguishing decals.

SIX OF THE BEST ON SALE AT A LOCAL DEALERSHIP

2014 VOLKSWAGEN CALIFORNIA SE 140 BMT £51,671

Fully functional kitchen with 2-burner hob, fridge and sink. Reclining bench bed, adjustable and tilting bed area. Sat nav. Colour screen touch-screen. Blown air heating, folding table, privacy glass, 12/230v electrical system. Electro-hydraulic pop-up roof, awning. 10 miles.

2014 HILLSIDE BIRCHOVER 2.0TDI 102PS HIGHLINE £40,995

The Birchover is a desirable 2 or 4 berth Camper with an abundance of style and sophistication. Specification includes: colour-coded bumpers and mirrors, cruise control, air conditioning, alloy wheels, reverse sensors. The living area is 2-berth but there is an option of an additional double bed in the roof. There is a fridge, cooking facilities, Eberspächer heating, hot water, porta-potti and on-board fresh water. 100 miles.

2013 JÖBL KAMPA SE SPORT 2.0TDI 102PS HIGHLINE £39,995

A high quality Camper with a specification that includes: metallic paint, colour-coded bumpers and mirrors, cruise control, air conditioning, 20in alloy wheels, 35mm suspension lowering kit, sill guards, reverse sensors and Bluetooth. There is a fridge, cooking facilities, Eberspächer heater, hot water, porta-potti and on-board fresh water. 17,064 miles

2013 LEISUREDRIVE CRUSADER 2.0-LITRE TDI 102PS HIGHLINE £36,995

A high quality Camper. Specification includes: metallic paint, colour-coded bumpers and mirrors, air conditioning, alloy wheels, reverse sensors, Bluetooth. The living area is 2-berth but there is an option of an additional bed in the roof. There is a fridge, cooking facilities, Eberspächer heater, hot water, porta-potti and on-board fresh water. Ex-demonstrator, 300 miles.

2008 CROMHALL CALIFORNIA 2.5TDI 130PS (LEFT-HAND-DRIVE) £27,995

4-berth Camper by Cromhall Refinishing Ltd of Bristol. Built to original specification using only original parts. Specification includes Electric pop-up roof system, blown-air heating system, 2-burner gas hob and sink. 42ltr fridge. Folding table. On-board fresh water tank. 75,000 miles

2008 LEISUREDRIVE CRUSADER 1.9TDI 84PS (POWER UPGRADE TO 102 PS) £23,750

Very rare automatic clutch model. Passenger safe swivel, wind-out awning, split-charging system, recently fitted timing belt, service history, cruise control, reversing sensors. Silver, 75,000 miles.

FIVE CONSECUTIVE YEARS OF 'HOME-INSTALLED' CAMPER CONVERSIONS BASED ON THE PRE-FACELIFT T5

2004 – VW T5 SWB CAMPER & EXTRAS   £24,950
T5 T28, 84,000 miles, full conversion in 2012. Reimo roof, Smart
¾ bed, Smev 2-ring hob and sink, Waeco fridge, four berth, swivel
double passenger seat, side bars, lowered springs, new turbo 2013,
Vango Airbeam Sapera standard awning with footprint and two carpets,
tailgate awning, double self-inflating bed, four-place dinner set including
cutlery. MoT.

2005 – VW T5   £15,000
T28 T5 Transporter, 98,000 miles. Barn doors. 12-months MoT. Excellent
condition inside and out. Waci fridge, Smev 2 burner hob with separate
Smev sink. ¾ rock 'n' roll bed in Inca to match front seats. 240v hook-up.
New leisure battery. Single swivel passenger seat. Removable table. This
has been remapped from 88PS to 110PS. Well worth a look.

2006 –VW T5 2.5TDI 174PS LWB   £19,000
54,000 miles. Stunning van with part conversion making this the ideal
versatile Camper. 4-berth Torbay Camper conversion. Reimo pop-top,
roof bed. Passenger and driver's swivel seats, leisure battery with
split-change relay 4 x 12v, 3 x 24v sockets. Hook-up, twin sliding doors.
LED stork roof reading lights, factory fitted window blinds, awning rail.

2007 – VW TRANSPORTER CAMPER VAN   £24,000
VW Transporter in Black, 82,000 miles. Full conversion with pop-top
roof. Excellent condition inside and out. Comes with 12 months MoT
and full service.

2008 – T5 CAMPER SWB 2.5 (130PS)   £27,000
Grey, A/C, E/W. One previous owner, 15,500 miles. MoT. Reimo roof,
rib seat, 18in alloys, Waeco fridge, 12v plus 230v. Electrics, Gas safety
certificate, Carbon Vofringer units, Smev cooker/sink. Fixed CAK water
tank, tinted windows, Single passenger seat and swivel. Stainless roof
bars, Van-x curtains. No outstanding finance.

FIVE EXAMPLES OF T5 DELIVERY OR WINDOW VANS, WHICH MIGHT BE SUITABLE FOR CONVERSION TO A CAMPER AS A HOME PROJECT

2004
Short wheelbase Kombi, 90,000 miles
– £9,495

2006
9 seater Transporter, 80,000 miles
– £12,000

2007
105PS Kombi, 164,000 miles
– £6,999

2007
Short wheelbase Van, 96,000 miles
– £7,999

2009
Short wheelbase van, 19,000 miles
– £9,999

CHAPTER 4
CLASSIC CONVERSIONS OUTLINED

To offer a comprehensive picture of all the classic Campers produced by conversion firms authorised or otherwise by Volkswagen would demand a book of over 100,000 words, more than 450 illustrations and 400 pages. If such a book proves marque expertise, the credentials offered by the author of this guide ensure that the matter has already been addressed fairly and squarely!

Here, however, the aim is to make use of that acquired knowledge and summarise with a selection of conversions for each generation, and in the case of the older models, particularly the first- and second-generation Transporters, those most likely to be seen at shows or up for grabs (at a price) on the market. With the slightly less loved T3, the decision has been taken to concentrate on the particularly well equipped and more likely rust-free, or less rusty, examples. For the T4 and the new versatility the chassis cab offered, the emphasis is placed on coachbuilt motorhome models, via a diversion to look at the weekender practicalities of Multivan ownership. Finally, for the T5, it would be rude not to place an emphasis on the VW California, Volkswagen's first factory-produced Camper, while also glancing at the product offered by one of the leading current day conversion companies.

➜ Cover of the 1959 brochure produced by Volkswagen to promote the Westfalia SO23.

1959–1967
FIRST-GENERATION CAMPERS

Two names dominate the current (British) scene, the German firm of Westfalia and Jack White's Sidmouth-based company and its brand name of Devon. However, there are sufficient examples of the work of the Canterbury Pitt operation out there for the 'moto caravan' also to be worthy of illustration.

As conversions by big name Dormobile only really come into abundance with the second-generation Transporter (despite their autumn 1961 for '62 VW debut) they can be overlooked. Instead, this section finishes with a glance towards the world of the US Campmobile, quite a few examples of which have made their largely rust-free way across the Atlantic.

WESTFALIA

The Westfalia-Werke, whose origins can be traced all the way back to 1844, carry a triple accolade. They were possibly the first to create a full Camper conversion, definitely the pioneer of the Camping Kit (a cabinet to pop in at a weekend and remove for the working week) and the definitive official 'partner' to Volkswagen, although this wasn't formalised until the last years of the 1950s. In all Volkswagen's dealings, the importance of the American market cannot be overplayed. Westfalia duly supplied Volkswagen of America with Campers and such was the demand that after a relatively short time US dealers had to commission local tradesmen to copy the German product with what some wags have since chosen to call Westfakias! These Campmobiles – the term could only be of American descent – which did indeed bear more than a passing resemblance to the genuine article, were conversions built on surplus stocks of Delivery Vans and Kombis, but that's a story too far, despite its fascination. With the support of the Campmobile, Westfalia's influence extended through much of mainland Europe and across America, continents where left-hand-drive vehicles were largely the norm. A handful of right-hand-drive examples (think South Africa and Australia) do exist, but the company's presence wasn't apparent in Great Britain until the 1970s.

By 1959, when Volkswagen produced its first official piece of print to promote 'The Volkswagen Camper with Westfalia De Luxe Equipment', Westfalia had revised its previous offerings into what was known as the SO23 in Germany and beyond. SO stands for *Sonderausführungen*, or special model, a term that emerged from the Transporter's adaptability for numerous uses and Volkswagen's desire to catalogue such vehicles, be they factory equipped and produced, the work of specialist coachbuilders *Karosserie*, or even little more than design ideas.

WESTFALIA SO23 1958–1961

If you want one of these, they can be found and, amazingly, quite often in remarkable condition. However, expect to pay big, big money and even more if the vehicle comes with all possible accessories. The accompanying images taken from the earliest SO23 brochure illustrate the layout of the SO23 by day and night, while also revealing some of the Westfalia conversion's most recognisable and endearing characteristics. Note particularly the wardrobe behind the rear side-loading door with its lovely rounded mirror glass, the plaid material used in all areas except the cab and, on a more trivial level, the

shell-shaped twin wall lamps. Only barely visible is the Plexiglas container balanced on the top of the kitchen/washroom cabinet, a box that holds four spun and coloured aluminium 6oz cups and six similarly formed shot glasses. Rumour has it that a second-mortgage figure is required to acquire such a set if it is missing and such a sum is indicative of missing SO23 accessories generally.

One final feature worthy of mention, and far from obvious in the illustrations, is the SO23's skylight, a standard feature bearing a passing resemblance to a submarine hatch and duly nicknamed thus.

← Day and night configurations illustrated in these delightful cutaway drawings of the SO23.

→ The SO23's attributes with measurements in inches (for the US market).

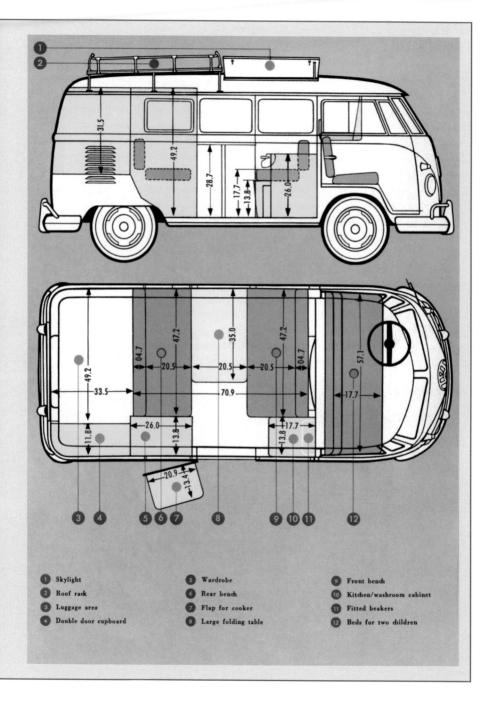

1. Skylight
2. Roof rack
3. Luggage area
4. Double door cupboard
5. Wardrobe
6. Rear bench
7. Flap for cooker
8. Large folding table
9. Front bench
10. Kitchen/washroom cabinet
11. Fitted beakers
12. Beds for two children

WESTFALIA SO34/35 1961–1964

While there might be a few more SO34 models about than there are SO23s, this Camper definitely comes under the general heading of a highly desirable rarity. A good example, and most of them that have survived are, will cost just as much as its illustrious predecessor.

Three snippets of information will elevate your knowledge towards anorak status. First, why is there a dual designation? The answer is straightforward; the SO34's cabinets (the more commonly seen of the two) are produced in white and grey laminate, while the SO35 has a dark Swiss pear wood finish. Second, both variations are known in enthusiast territory as the 'flip-seat' Camper. This is because the backrest of the cab bench seat could be 'flipped' (via substantial supports) through 180 degrees to form an integral part of the Camper's interior, and in the process create a living area larger than had been possible previously. Third, as illustrated here, the earlier SO34/35 brochure cover ranks as one of the most famous, truly iconic images of Volkswagen's air-cooled era, and if that wasn't enough, the final version (entitled 'Is it a Boat?') has to be the quirkiest!

Study the layout and the flexibility contained in the design and you will see that here was a Camper at the head of the pack and possibly ahead of its time.

➔ Layout illustrations for the SO34 and SO35.

⬇ Surely the most iconic brochure cover to emerge from the Volkswagen stable – the SO34.

VW Camping Car 34 and VW Camping Car 35

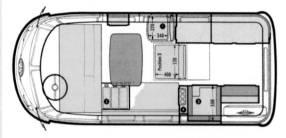

(Underway)

1 Folding chair

2 Three two-gallon water cans

3 Two cu. ft. ice box

4 »Bar« with shelf for beakers

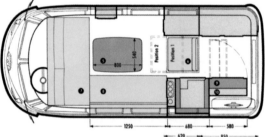

(Stationary)

5 Table

6 Sliding seat

7 Upholstered seat bench

8 Upholstered seat bench

9 Petrol cooker

10 Kitchen cabinet – swinging

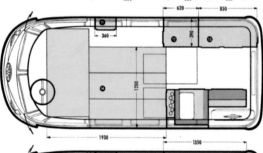

(Without beds for children)

11 Washing and shaving cabinet

12 Wardrobe

13 Linen cupboard

14 Beds for adults

(With beds for children)

15 Child's bed (hammock)

16 Sleeping accommodation for second child

17 Stowage room for tent

18 Stowage room on top of ice box

19 Table support for use with spare

WESTFALIA SO42 1965–1967

Without doubt, someone keen to part with their money will find more examples of the SO42 on offer than either of its predecessors. Of course, this state of affairs is the same across the board with the first-generation Transporter; the later the year of manufacture, the more examples are available to be snapped up.

The most instantly recognisable feature of the SO42 is its pop-top roof, banishing the days of the submarine hatch as outdated technology. The accompanying layout plan illustrates its diminutive nature, while also drawing attention to the fact that the SO42 was available as both a bulkhead and walkthrough model.

In America the SO42 was openly branded as the Campmobile, while in mainland Europe this conversion was joined by the less popular SO44, a Camper with a substantial unit to the rear of the bulkhead.

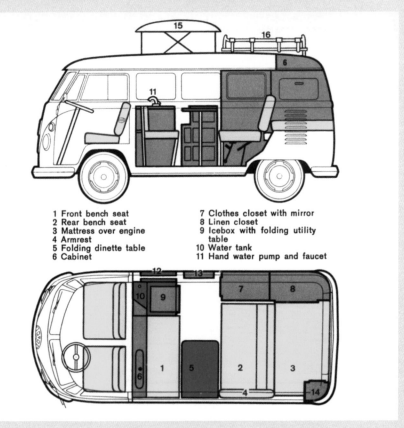

1 Front bench seat
2 Rear bench seat
3 Mattress over engine
4 Armrest
5 Folding dinette table
6 Cabinet

7 Clothes closet with mirror
8 Linen closet
9 Icebox with folding utility table
10 Water tank
11 Hand water pump and faucet

➜ Cover of the home-market brochure produced to promote the SO42 (1965–1967).

⬇ The layout of the SO42 – note the pop-up top (partially masked in the cover illustration.

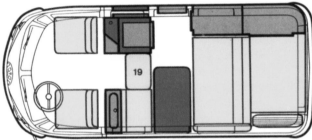

12 Folding utility table on right side door
13 Shelf cabinet on left side door
14 Corner cabinet in rear (not available in split front seat version)
15 Pop-up top (optional extra)

16 Roof rack (optional extra)
17 Child's hammock
18 Rear bench seat converted to double bed
19 Removable jump seat (only available in split front seat version)

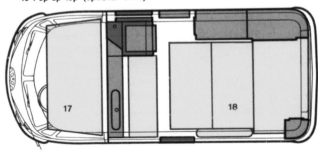

DEVON

Jack White was a highly successful builder based in the delightful seaside resort of Sidmouth in Devon. As his young family expanded, his days of travelling across Europe to visit his wife's relatives in a Beetle were strictly numbered. As the last months of 1955 gave way to the first of the following year, Jack set about the task of designing an interior for his newly acquired and much more spacious VW Transporter. With the help of master craftsman Pat Mitchell (Jack's designer and builder of kitchen units), a bespoke camping interior was slotted into the Transporter. Four carefully constructed seats and a table with a laminate top quickly converted to a double divan in the central section of the Transporter, while a single bed was added over the engine bay and another crossways, utilising the front seats.

A little later a fifth bed was added, which with considerable ingenuity was suspended above the bottom end of the double divan. The complete makeover from Delivery Van to Camper included the installation of a cooker, basic washing facilities (deemed perfectly adequate in their day), an Osokool storage cabinet (a precursor to today's state-of-the-art fridges), fitted cupboards and, of course, Calor gas and 6V DC electricity. Soft furnishings came in the form of luxury Dunlopillo cushions and neatly fitting curtains.

From this one vehicle and the attention it attracted was born J.P. White (Sidmouth) Ltd, makers of Camper vans. Jack, a proud Devonian, born and bred, inevitably selected the brand name

THE CRAFTSMANSHIP OF A CURVED CABINET

The earliest of Devon conversions featured a beautiful hand-built, curved cabinet, which was located to the rear of the side loading doors. The arrival of the 1961 model (in the final months of 1960) saw the solid-oak curved cabinet, which had initially been home to the two-burner cooker and latterly for its storage when the vehicle was on the move, replaced with a cheaper square-edged unit. Fortunately, a few curved cabinets have survived and perhaps it is testament to the design and its beauty that many modern craftsmen are commissioned to replicate this unit in bespoke conversions carried out on classic models.

BEWARE THE DEVONETTE AND THE TORVETTE?

For 1962 Devon introduced what was known as the Devonette. Four years later this model was replaced by the Torvette. Although the word 'budget' wasn't used, this is what both models were. The opening text of the generic 1962 brochure gives the game away: 'Here is a Motorised Caravan in the lower price range that offers all that is necessary for both your leisure hours and your everyday travelling needs.'

A descriptive pricelist issued in the same year goes some way to explain why the Devonette could be sold at a cheaper price. Whereas the Caravette was described as being finished 'in hand-polished Natural Oak', the Devonette was simply offered in 'Natural Oak Woodwork'. The difference was even more obvious when mahogany was the chosen wood. For the Caravette the wording read, 'hand-polished mahogany', but for

the Devonette this was amended to 'Mahogany colour woodwork with natural oak side panels'.

The Devonette and Torvette models were of a lower material specification and also lacked some of the equipment that was a standard feature of the Caravette, in essence a deluxe and a standard model, or as the years went by more and more so a fully fledged Camper and a people carrier that could double as a weekender.

Realistically, most purchasers will prefer the archaic charms of the Caravette, but some remarkably fine examples of base-model Devon Campers and similar models from other converters are in existence, often attracting considerable interest when they are displayed in or among a line-up of first-generation Campers, or shown in a concours competition.

of Devon, but with further ingenuity, christened the conversion the Caravette. Within the space of a few short years and several changes of premises, each one successively larger, by 1960 Devon was producing in the region of 1,000 vehicles per year and employed 75 workers.

Numbers continued to increase, the direct result of a reputation built on quality and craftsmanship linked to the quasi-official status bestowed on the company by Volkswagen ('Fully approved by Volkswagenwerk in Germany and VW Motors Ltd. Volkswagen Concessionaires for Great Britain'). Sadly, Jack White suffered a fatal heart attack at the age of 51 in November 1963. Predictably, the company was sold the following year, its purchasers being the Renwick, Wilton and Dobson Group, but it was a good number of years, and under changing circumstances in Britain and beyond, before the standards imposed by Jack were revised.

THE DEVON CARAVETTE (1963 SPECIFICATION)

As might be anticipated, the specification of the Devon Caravette was subject to near continual improvement, with the changes for the following year being announced at the annual Earls Court Motor Show held in the autumn of the current one. For example, in October 1965, for 1966 models, Devon added walk-through options to their line-up, or in other words, Campers where the driver and front-seat passenger could

manoeuvre themselves directly from the cab to the main 'living area' without getting out of the vehicle. Clearly, not an option with the bulkhead model, which was still on offer, Devon christened the walk-through versions as 'Spaceway' models.

The 1963 Devon Caravette has been chosen to represent first-generation Transporter conversions for two reasons. Part of the brochure text is devoted to

The DEVON CARAVETTE

MOTORISED CARAVAN

⬇ Devon presented the specification for the following year by October of the current one. Sadly, when colour covers were introduced (this '1963' offering is one of the first) such luxury was not extended to the interior pages.

IGNED AND

DUCED BY

ON CRAFTSMEN

THE

KSWAGEN

RO BUS

JIATIO

4 CT 1962

(W) BRARY

Fully approved by

KSWAGENWERK

in Germany

and

. MOTORS LTD.

swagen Concessionaires for
Great Britain

what, Devon would have argued, set them aside from most other operations, namely quality guaranteed. More significantly, the brochure was the first one in the series to carry a full-colour cover. Devon Caravettes of 1963 vintage are definitely out there on the market although a good one won't be cheap. See what accolades of a bygone age you would be inheriting:

A Home in the Country and always A Fine Motor Car

Your Devon Caravette assures you of comfort and elegance. The hand-polished natural oak finish of the craftsman-made woodwork combined with the luxury of the fabrics equal the fine quality of the vehicle to which they are fitted ... The best quality materials are used in the conversion and the fitted curtains, 'Duracou' seat covers on deep foam cushions, 'Formica'-topped tables, and 'Polyfloor' tiles, emphasise the hard-wearing qualities of this superb motorised caravan.

Devon Caravette Specification

Cooking facilities: Two-burner cooker with grill, complete with grill pan

Cooking Medium: Bottled gas from either of both of two points

Storage: Lockers under both seats, one with heater. Five small cupboards. Two large drawers. Soft garment storage under roof.

Cooler: 'Easicool' water evaporation food storage cabinet

Crockery: Four each, beakers, plates and fruit plates

Cutlery: Four each, knives forks, dessert spoons and teaspoons

Tables: Two, both adaptable for outside use and 'Formica' topped

Flooring: 'Polyfloor' tiles, in choice of colours, on resin-bonded ply under-surface

Woodwork: Hand polished natural oak

Water Supply: 11-gallon baffled tank, with drain-off plug, supplying 'whale' pump with built-in Perspex sink units

Seats: Deep foam cushions with 'Duracour' zipped covers in choice of colours

Curtains: In choice of colours, on nylon runners and alloy rail

Side Awning: Lightweight Continental canvas with poles, pegs and guy ropes

Lighting: Fluorescent light, plus two other electric lights

CANTERBURY PITT

A good number of Canterbury Pitt conversions have survived and are generally regarded as being among the best, partly due to the quality of the workmanship involved and undoubtedly to the versatility of the layout.

Early brochures make no reference to 'Canterbury' as it wasn't until 1961 that Peter Pitt merged with Canterbury Sidecars Ltd, who, despite their name, were based in South Ockendon, Romford, rather than Kent. Production of what was rather clumsily labelled latterly as

THE 'PITT OPEN PLAN'

Seating arrangements:
1) Eight large seats for adults, six forward facing, six window seats. This is the normal travelling arrangement.

2) Clear floor-space for the carriage of bulky packages or belongings. So you may load and unload with ease.

3) Combined seating and floor-space with room for movement or carriage of large items.
[Note that] the main table can be set up outside for six people so that they can cook and enjoy the company and the good weather.

Yes, a place for everything and everything in the right place. Study the pictures on this page and see how everything is near to hand when you want it. From the time you wake to the delights of sizzling bacon and eggs until you heave the last contented sigh as you snuggle down with your bedtime cocoa . sheer luxury

Fold-away two ring cooker-griller for indoor and hot day out-door use.

Fitted crockery and cutlery for four optional (Kombi two-ring cooker).

Fold-away Drainer-sink (optional on all models.)

FRONT VIEW
"Special" equipment now standard on Micro bus (optional extra on Kombi).

SO

seats 8

so that you can enjoy the scenery without feeling cramped in any way Relax on the deep foam cushions which have detachable covers in a choice of colours. Ideal for the children too, plenty of room to bounce about without tiring adult passengers—there's space for teddy and the favourite dolls as well.

SEATING ARRANGEMENTS
Plan 1
Eight large seats for adults six forward facing six window seats This is the normal travelling arrangement.
Clear floorspace for the carriage of bulky packages or belongings. So you may load and unload with ease.
Plan 3
Combined seating and floorspace with room for movement or carriage of large items.
The main table can be set up outside for six people so that you can cook and enjoy the company and the good weather

THE "PITT

REAR VIEW

Clear Floor Space

'The Canterbury Volkswagen Pitt open plan Moto-Caravan' escalated nicely through the remaining years of first-generation Transporter production and seemed set to continue apace in the succeeding Bay era. Sadly, this was not to be, as Peter Pitt died in February 1969. His arrangement with Canterbury was such that all conversions were made under licence, a contract that expired on his demise. As such, although a few Canterbury Pitt Bays appear to date to the immediate period after his death, by the autumn of 1969, the Pitt concept was no more. A second generation 'Open Plan' is a rare beast indeed.

Sleeping:

Beds for adults

Plan a) A roomy double bed size 4ft x 6ft

Plan b) A single bed size 3ft x 6ft

Plan c) Twin beds 2ft x 6ft (optional additional bed for child or adult)

Beds for children

Children's berths in car and rear (making use of the space over the engine compartment and the cab seat)

Everyone has room to sleep and will wake completely refreshed

← Centre spread from Canterbury Pitt's 1967 foldout style brochure.

↑ Internal page from
Volkswagen of America's
'Send this kit to camp'
brochure of 1962.

THE CAMPMOBILE (OR WESTFAKIA)

There was a big problem in early 1960s America. Westfalia couldn't keep up with the demand for their products and the US dealers were far from happy. To make matters worse, so rumour has it, sales of Delivery Vans and Pick-ups were in the doldrums, or in American parlance 'rot lot'. Dirty deeds lay ahead as it appears probable that VW of America (VWoA) insisted dealers took unwanted Delivery Vans etc. if they were to have any hope of being allocated a consignment of Campers. According to those who wish to paint officialdom as black as black, the dealers had little option but to club together and commission the fledgling firm Sportsmobile to create Campers with more than a passing resemblance to the genuine German article. A more charitable interpretation would be that it was VWoA who initiated such works. Whichever, the Campmobile was born as the cover of an atypical brochure from the time reveals.

What is probably of most interest to those contemplating the purchase of either a Westfalia model of the era, or the US 'copies', is a few lines of the text from the decidedly dull and uninspiringly covered brochure from 1962 entitled 'Which body types make good campers?'. Here, the concept of building, or having built, your own Camper from a vehicle you already own or can afford to buy is taken to a logical extreme, while also providing a fascinating insight into what today's owner might expect to find in the specification of a 1960s model.

WHICH BODY TYPES MAKE GOOD CAMPERS?

The VW Panel Truck, The VW Kombi Station Wagon, The VW Deluxe Station Wagon, The VW Standard Station Wagon

... These four Volkswagens were not designed primarily for camping out. But they do do double duty when equipped with special Volkswagen fittings ... If you're thinking of buying one of these Volkswagens, you can order it completely equipped. If you already own one, you can have the equipment installed at any time.

Camp equipment for the VW Panel Truck (option Texas 500, sold complete at $730.00)

- Ice box cabinet with ice box and water tank
- Vanity cabinet with mirror
- Medicine cabinet, left side
- Front seat without cushions
- Rear seat without cushions, with toilet
- Ceiling panels (set of 4)
- Left wall panel
- Left door panel
- Right door panel
- Floor panels (set)
- Bed boards (2)
- Table with leg and hinge, 24in x 30in
- Table (door), 15in x 20in
- Cushions (set of 8)
- Curtains (set)
- Stove, two-burner LP gas

Other camp equipment for the VW Kombi and the VW Panel Truck (option number: West K-22, sold complete at $984.00)

Windows (5) gear operation – with garnish and drip cap

Folding table with 'Getalit' top attached to the frame between the two benches

Two benches (front and rear) with removable cushions and backrests, converting into double bed

Two wedge-shaped head rests

Floor covering and rug

Drapes for all windows in the living room

Rod and drapes between the driver's cab and living compartment

Large side tent with poles and attachments, 8.9ft L x 5.3ft W x 6.7ft H

Wardrobe with inside mirror, 26.3in L x 15.7in W x 50.4in H

Linen Closet, 31in L x 12.6in W x 31.5in H

Ice Box that holds 14½ gallons ice

Hammock for child's sleeping accommodation

Washing cabinet at right-hand door wing

Roof rack 53in L x 56in W x 18in H, 220lb. payload

Drop-leaf table at left-hand door wing for stove, 20.9in x 13.4in

Chemical toilet (with one box of chemicals)

Two-burner gasoline stove

Electric roof lamp, cable, plug and socket

Three 2½ gallon water canisters, stowed in the chest underneath the front bench

Plastic washbowl in lower compartment of washing bowl

* The astute will detect that the Texas version comprises the essential ingredients to turn a Delivery Van into a Campmobile, or Westfakia, while the West option embraces many elements of a genuine Westfalia model.

1967–1979
SECOND-GENERATION CAMPERS

Examples abound on British driveways of both Westfalia and Devon second-generation Campers, as do conversions from both Dormobile and, relatively new boys on the scene, Danbury. Possibly one of the most interesting models though has to be the Camper branded as the Continental. Kitted out by Westfalia, but to a right-hand-drive configuration, two versions bearing such a name were marketed and sold under the Devon umbrella.

WESTFALIA OPTIONS 1971

By 1971, Westfalia were offering no less than six conversions. However, scrutiny of the name bestowed on each model quickly reveals that three were intended for the European market, while the rest were for US dealers. While some variations in specification can be readily detected (most notably the absence of a grill/cooker in all US versions), it is also quite easy to pair each European market model with its American equivalent. As the accompanying image of the European layouts illustrates, all three options carried a reasonably high specification, although the Helsinki lacked some of the equipment offered on the other two models.

- SO72/1 Camper Luxembourg
- SO72/2 Camper Los Angeles
- SO72/3 Camper Helsinki
- SO72/4 Camper Houston
- SO72/5 Camper Madrid
- SO72/6 Camper Miami

With the arrival of new Westfalia conversions for the second-generation Transporter, there also came a new style of elevating roof and one that makes identifying Campers from the German firm easy (although both the Martin Walter/Dormobile roof and the pop-top linked to the previous generation SO42, were still available).

The new roof took the form of a full-length white fibreglass top. At its rear was a built-in roof rack, complete with longitudinal rods to ensure luggage didn't foul the Camper's roof panel. The elevating section occupied the remainder, with hinges at the front end of the vehicle, ensuring that when in use, the maximum extra height available was over the centre of the vehicle.

The autumn of 1973 saw a revision to the roof arrangements with the 'roof rack being transferred to the front of the vehicle' and the hinges of the pushed-back elevating section being reversed, so that they were at the rear. This afforded maximum available height to taller owners in the crucial area behind the cab-seats, a part of the vehicle where cookers and sinks were most likely to be found.

WESTFALIA

Assembly of the 30,000th Westfalia Camper was completed on 30 March 1968, while 14 months later, in May 1969, a further 20,000 conversions had been added to the grand total. Significantly, the 50,000th conversion was destined for the United States. By 1968, a massive 75 per cent of Westfalia's production was intended for export, the majority share of which was bound for America. The big day came in 1971 when the 100,000th conversion rolled of the assembly line, by which time of the 22,417 Campers built during the year, in the region of 19,000, or 84 per cent of the daily production of 125 vehicles, were destined for the USA.

⬇ Layouts offered to Westfalia's home-market customers in 1971 – Madrid, Luxemburg and Helsinki.

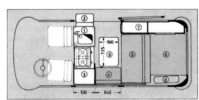

Einrichtung Typ Madrid
1 Vorratsschrank mit 50-l-Isolierbox, Spülbecken mit 28-l-Wassertank und Handpumpe, Staufach und Abdeckplatte
2 Waschregal mit seitlichem Klapptisch
3 Kleiderschrank mit Spiegel, 2-flammiger, versenkbarer Propangaskocher mit Anschluß an 2 5-kg-Gasflaschen im Kleiderschrank

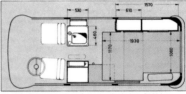

4 seitliche Polstersitzbank mit Stauraum, abnehmbare Rücklehne
5 hintere Polstersitzbank mit Stauraum
6 Polster auf dem Motorraum, im Dach Staukasten
7 Mehrzweckschrank
8 Reserveradverkleidung
9 schwenkbarer Eßtisch

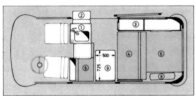

Einrichtung Typ Luxemburg
1 Vorratsschrank mit 50-l-Isolierbox, Spülbecken mit 28-l-Wassertank und Handpumpe, Staufach und Abdeckplatte
2 Waschregal mit seitlichem Klapptisch
3 Doppelschrank mit Spiegel für Kleider und Wäsche
4 hintere Polstersitzbank mit Stauraum

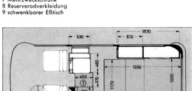

5 vordere Polstersitzbank mit Stauraum
6 Polster auf dem Motorraum, im Dach Staukasten
7 gepolsterter Hocker
8 Reserveradverkleidung
9 abklappbarer Eßtisch

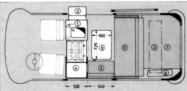

Einrichtung Typ Helsinki
1 Vorratsschrank mit 50-l-Isolierbox, Spülbecken mit 28-l-Wassertank und Handpumpe, Staufach und Abdeckplatte
2 Waschregal mit seitlichem Klapptisch
3 Hängeschrank für Wäsche über dem Motorraum
4 Kleiderschrank mit Spiegel, 2-flammiger, versenkbarer Propangas-

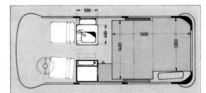

kocher mit Anschluß an 2 5-kg-Gasflaschen im Kleiderschrank
5 seitliche Polstersitzbank mit Stauraum, abnehmbare Rücklehne
6 hintere Polstersitzbank mit Stauraum
7 Polster auf dem Motorraum
8 Reserveradverkleidung
9 schwenkbarer Eßtisch

As a logical extension of this production boom, Westfalia increased the number of conversions available, deliberately tweaking the specification of certain models to satisfy the demands of Campmobile buyers.

Sadly, the seemingly impenetrable bubble burst in 1973, a time of recurrent oil crises, Middle East tensions and most notably a rapid souring of western economies by damaging inflation. Almost overnight, sales were down by a dramatic 35 per cent. Volkswagen of America had little option but to turn the tap off as far as home-grown Campmobiles were concerned, while the VW boss of the time, Rudolph Leiding, stopped production of the Transporter at the Emden factory and cut output at the original Hanover plant.

THE VW CONTINENTAL

Nothing in life is ever simple (at least where Camper conversions are concerned). Two successive models were marketed as the VW Continental. The first was a right-hand-drive adaptation of the Helsinki. The second was a right-hand-drive edition of the Malaga, introduced in September 1973. The Continental name survived until the debut of the rarely seen, if even heard of, Westfalia Oxford in 1976, close to the end of Devon's special relationship era.

From Volkswagen's own brochure, where 'The Volkswagen Continental' sat alongside 'The Volkswagen Caravette' not a word was mentioned relating either product to Westfalia or Devon:

It will comfortably carry six people ... For meal times you have a dining table with seating for four and room for a stool or highchair at the end. The meals are prepared on a well designed fold-away stainless steel cooker ... This is located next to the matching stainless steel wash basin, which is fitted with drain and stopper. Water is supplied via an easily operated pump.

When not in use the cooker folds away and the wash basin becomes a work surface. All work surfaces are heat and scratch resistant laminated plastic, which is easy to keep clean. ... On the side of the cooker is located a small utility table, which when folded down becomes a cover for the grocery shelf compartment. ... Bulky blankets, linen and toys are stored beneath the rear seats and in the wide overhead shelf across the upper floor. A full length wardrobe fitted with a mirrored door takes good care of those suits and dresses.

The walls and ceiling are all finished in wood grained birch plywood. Both are fibreglass insulated to protect against heating and cold. Wall to wall polyvinyl flooring is backed with felt soundproofing.

There are two large louvred and screened windows. Curtains which match the upholstery go all the way around for complete privacy.

And when it's time for bed there is no problem, 10 seconds sees the back seat folded out flat forming a full double bed. A child's bunk turns the driving compartment

By 1975, the shoots of recovery were apparent. For modern-day buyers, the result was that Westfalia had survived the storm, but in so doing had trimmed their range back to just two models, a policy that remained in place to the end of second-generation Transporter production. Fortunately, the Helsinki and Berlin models both offer a good specification, well worthy of consideration.

By the end of the 1960s, Volkswagen in the UK had given official approved status to a trio of converters. Inevitably, Devon headed the list; the other players were Dormobile and Danbury (more of which later). In 1972, a year during which they produced 3,500 conversions, Devon were afforded the privilege of being the sole UK converter to

⬇ If you want a right-hand-drive second-generation Westfalia Camper, the Continental is your option. Beware though, there are two (left pre-September '73 and right the later layout based on the Malaga).

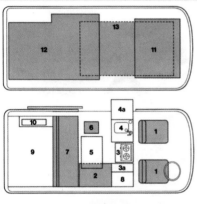

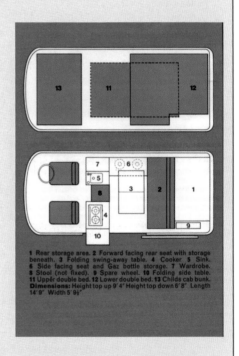

1 Individual front seats. 2 Side facing bench seat with storage compartment beneath. 3 Two ringed foldaway cooker unit. 3a Cooker unit housing (When cooker not in use). 4 Stainless steel sink unit. A twin-sided plastic laminated sink cover hinges out to become a working surface (4a). A utility table is fixed to the sink side hinging out beneath the working surface and an insulated food container is fitted below the sink itself. 5 Multi position dining table. 6 Free standing stool. 7 Front facing bench seat with storage space and camping gaz container beneath. 8 Clothes wardrobe with mirrored door 9 Rear storage area. 10 Covered spare wheel. 11 Childs bunk in drivers compartment. 12 Table (5) folds away and bench seat (7) extends to form a double bed. 13 6′ long double bed for two people situated in the pop-up top. (Indicated by dotted line).
Dimensions: Height top up 9′4″ Height top down 6′8″ Length 14′10″ Width 5′8″

1 Rear storage area. 2 Forward facing rear seat with storage beneath. 3 Folding swing-away table. 4 Cooker 5 Sink. 6 Side facing seat and Gaz bottle storage. 7 Wardrobe. 8 Stool (not fixed). 9 Spare wheel. 10 Folding side table. 11 Upper double bed. 12 Lower double bed. 13 Childs cab bunk.
Dimensions: Height top up 9′4″ Height top down 6′8″ Length 14′9″ Width 5′9½″

into another bedroom. Of course we still have the six foot long double bed for two people in the pop-up top, this is fitted as standard equipment. An interior neon tube ensures plenty of light inside even when it's dark outside.

Also standard with the Volkswagen Continental is the superbly designed 6ft 6in x 9ft 8in free standing side tent ...

Actually when you come to think about it, the Continental turns a little space into a lot of room.

'ICH BIN EIN BERLINER'

Three levels of Campmobile, all based on the Berlin, were offered when the conversion was introduced in the final months of 1975.

1. Standard Campmobile (P21)
- Stainless steel sink with electric water pump and utensil cabinet under opposite side loading door and with 7½ gallon water tank adjacent
- Icebox with storage bin adjacent
- Clothes closet with three storage areas adjacent
- Rear lid insect screen
- Ceiling cabinet over engine compartment
- Fluorescent ceiling lamp over ice box and storage bin
- Louvered windows on side of vehicle with side loading door
- Upholstered rear bench (with storage locker beneath) converts to double bed
- Dining table fore of rear bench
- Passenger seat in cab swivels
- Child's hammock arrangement over cab seats

2. Pop-up Top Campmobile (P22)
- As per P21 but with Westfalia's rear hinged elevating roof

3. Deluxe Campmobile (P27)
- As per P22 but with the following additional features:
- Between the cab seats manoeuvrable snack table
- Between the cab seats upholstered storage container
- Two burner stove added to the sink unit
- City water hook up
- 12-volt refrigerator (replacing the ice box)
- Fire extinguisher by the side of the rear bench seat on the same side as the side loading door

➜ Many rust-free late-model second-generation Campers turn out to be a Campmobile (based on the Westfalia Berlin). Volkswagen of America conveniently provided layout details.

be licensed by Volkswagen AG. The benefits included: the might of Volkswagen's marketing machine (for which read, among other things, specially designed and printed brochures), a full VW warranty on all of its products and service rights. In return, proving the point that nothing in life is free, Devon were expected to promote a model not from their stable as an integral part of the range. This model was the Continental, initially a right-hand-drive version of the Westfalia SO72/3 Helsinki. For modern-day owners reluctant to drive a vehicle with a steering wheel on the 'wrong' side, here is the opportunity to drive a genuine Westfalia model with ease.

More than a reasonable number of modern-day purchases of

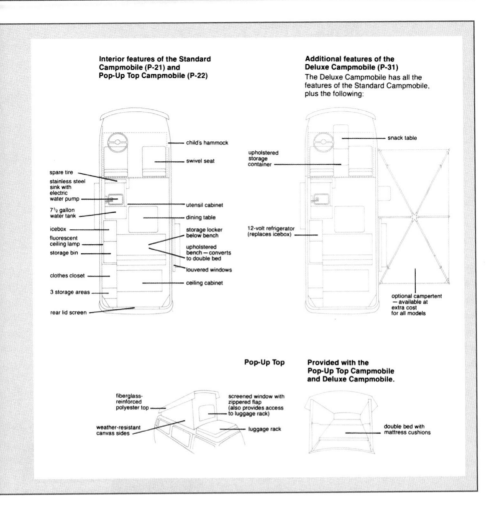

Interior features of the Standard
Campmobile (P-21) and
Pop-Up Top Campmobile (P-22)

Additional features of the
Deluxe Campmobile (P-31)
The Deluxe Campmobile has all the
features of the Standard Campmobile,
plus the following:

child's hammock
swivel seat
spare tire
stainless steel
sink with
electric
water pump
7½ gallon
water tank
icebox
fluorescent
ceiling lamp
storage bin
clothes closet
3 storage areas
rear lid screen
utensil cabinet
dining table
storage locker
below bench
upholstered
bench — converts
to double bed
louvered windows
ceiling cabinet

upholstered
storage
container
12-volt refrigerator
(replaces icebox)
snack table
optional campertent
— available at
extra cost
for all models

Pop-Up Top

**Provided with the
Pop-Up Top Campmobile
and Deluxe Campmobile.**

fiberglass-
reinforced
polyester top
weather-resistant
canvas sides
screened window with
zippered flap
(also provides access
to luggage rack)
luggage rack
double bed with
mattress cushions

second-generation Westfalias hail from the rust-free USA and some
particularly stunning examples of later versions have been snapped up
in recent years. What people have bought, despite the Campmobile
branding, is more or less the same as the model known in Europe as
the Berlin (an example of which is described and 'valued' in the chapter
concerning budgets). The Berlin, given the designation SO76/1, made
its debut in the autumn of 1975 as a '76 model.

In what was Westfalia's now slimmed-down itinerary of vehicles,
the Berlin was partnered by the Helsinki, a new version of the model
already discussed more than once. Introduced in the autumn of 1974 for
the '75 model year, the latest Helsinki carried the designation SO73/7.

DEVON

The era of the second-generation Transporter would briefly see Devon extend its range to three models, subsequently downgrade the Volkswagen 'donor' vehicle to either VW Kombi and eventually VW Delivery Van status, and abandon its commitment to hand-polished oak in favour of laminates and veneers. Confusingly, names were used once and later re-issued offering a different specification. While the Devonette and Torvette of first-generation Transporter days were quite clearly budget models, Devon wavered between offering an obvious weekender and a Camper with a good specification, if not one quite in the same league as the top-of-the-range model of the same year/s.

On the assumption that most buyers hunting for a classic Devon would select one offering the highest specification possible for the given year, the examples that follow are an early Eurovette and the late Moonraker, both top-of-the-range examples at the time of their introduction.

⬇ The Eurovette (that's the cooker unit on view through the sliding door) was, as the interior image illustrates, a model worthy of top-of-the-range status.

DEVON MODELS YEAR BY YEAR (SECOND GENERATION)

YEAR	FULLY FLEDGED CAMPER	FULLY FLEDGED CAMPER	BUDGET MODEL OR WEEKENDER
1968–1970	Eurovette Based on the VW Micro Bus	Caravette (lower spec than the Eurovette) based on the VW Micro Bus	Torvette Based on the VW Kombi
1971	Moonraker 1) Based on the VW Micro Bus 2) Lower cost, based on the VW Kombi		Sunlander 1) Based on the VW Micro Bus 2) Lower cost, based on the VW Kombi
1972	Moonraker 1) Based on the VW Micro Bus 2) Lower cost, based on the VW Kombi		Devonette 1) Based on the VW Micro Bus 2) Lower cost, based on the VW Kombi
1973	Moonraker 1) Based on the VW Micro Bus 2) Lower cost, based on the VW Kombi	Caravette 1) Micro Bus 2) Kombi. The latest incarnation of the Caravette carried many of the luxury features of a fully fledged Camper while retaining the necessary flexibility to act as a weekender or convenient people carrier during the week.	
1974–1975	Eurovette Based on the VW Kombi. With or without elevating roof	Caravette Based on the VW Kombi. With or without elevating roof	
1976	Eurovette With flat or elevating roof, based on the VW Kombi	Devonette De Luxe model incl. elevating roof, based on the Kombi Standard model, with or without elevating roof, based on the Delivery Van	
1977	Eurovette With flat or elevating roof based on the VW Kombi With flat or elevating roof based on the Delivery Van	Devonette De Luxe model with or without elevating roof based on the Kombi Standard model with or without elevating roof based on the Delivery Van	
1978	Moonraker With flat or elevating roof, based on the VW Kombi		Sundowner With flat or elevating roof, based on the Delivery Van
1979	Moonraker With flat or elevating roof, based on the VW Kombi	Sundowner With flat or elevating roof based on the Delivery Van – note, the specification of the Sundowner had been amended to offer a more comprehensive package of camping equipment	

Also, note the introduction of a new style elevating roof known as the 'Double-top'. Offering two solid base bed sections, which could be combined to produce a double bed 6ft 1in long by 3ft 9in wide. Double-top models can be identified by the bulk of the roof panel, resulting in the vehicle having an overall height of 6ft 11½in compared to the flat roof model's 6ft 5in, or 6ft 9in (in parts) with the standard elevating roof.

'GETTING DOWN TO DETAILS ...' DEVON MOONRAKER 1978/79

VW Devon Moonraker built on VW Kombi with deluxe cab trim including brushed nylon seats with head restraints.

Interior trim and floor

■ Rich carpet trim covers all interior panels up to window level.

■ A removable toning brown carpet overlays an attractive brown and cream patterned vinyl floor with polystyrene insulation underneath.

Seating

■ There is a 2/3 seater rear bench seat, with ample storage beneath.

■ A single rear-facing upright seat is fixed to the face of the wardrobe. An additional single seat is provided, so that it can be easily converted to a double bench seat for dining.

■ The rear bench seat pulls out easily to form a large double bed. The rear seat and engine deck cushions provide a deep foam mattress.

⊛ Devon

MOONRAKER

The Moonraker is a brand new motor caravan built on the famous VW Kombi.

There's dozens of refinements on board to make you feel at home wherever you are.

Lots of storage space, large cool box (optional fridge), cooker, grill, underfloor water storage, carpet and deluxe cab trim to name but a few.

And if you can drive a car – you can drive a VW Devon.

It handles and parks just like a family saloon.

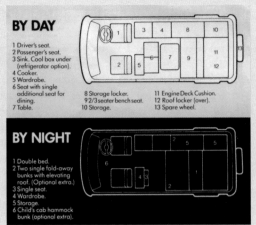

BY DAY

1 Driver's seat.
2 Passenger's seat.
3 Sink. Cool box under (refrigerator option).
4 Cooker.
5 Wardrobe.
6 Seat with single additional seat for dining.
7 Table.
8 Storage locker.
9 2/3 seater bench seat.
10 Storage.
11 Engine Deck Cushion.
12 Roof locker (over).
13 Spare wheel.

BY NIGHT

1 Double bed.
2 Two single fold-away bunks with elevating roof. (Optional extra.)
3 Single seat.
4 Wardrobe.
5 Storage.
6 Child's cab hammock bunk (optional extra).

← 'A brand new' Moonraker (Devon tended to reuse names). As the layout plan confirms, all the units were located down one side of the vehicle.

Kitchen and Storage units

■ A complete kitchen and storage unit is fitted along the offside of the vehicle. This includes stainless steel sink and drainer with faucet, electric water pump, and double burner with grill and built-in splash guard.

■ Beneath the sink is a large cool box (optional fridge). Below the cooker are two pull-out drawers, one for cutlery, and a roomy double cupboard.

■ To the right of the cooker is a large storage locker with a hinged flap top, with gas bottle storage cupboard beneath, vented to the outside.

■ On the offside of the engine deck is a useful upright storage cupboard with 3 cubbyhole shelves at the back, and above, a roof locker with a hinged front.

■ Behind the passenger's seat is an upright hanging wardrobe with access doors on both sides.

Table

■ Table is stored under the roof locker and when in use is fixed on a single column leg in the centre of the floor area.

■ There is an interior fluorescent light.

Water storage

■ A 7-gallon capacity under-floor water tank is fitted.

Spare Wheel

■ The spare wheel is on a mounting bracket fitted to a hinged cradle and fixed externally above the rear bumper, and protected by a fitted vinyl cover.

Cushions and Curtains

■ Attractive buttoned deep foam cushions in a brown and beige check material with printed floral pattern curtains running on a continuous curtain track.

Windows

■ Four large windows in passenger area and the offside front has a double louvre for fresh air ventilation.

DEVON MOTOR CARAVANS – 1969, EUROVETTE

Conversion on the 1600cc Volkswagen Micro Bus with 'Spaceway' access. Finished in natural oak with fabrics, floor tiles and tabletop in blending colours. Fitted with plastic washable insulated headlining, side panelling, fluorescent electric light, oven cooker unit, cab passenger headrest, fire extinguisher, wheel trims, crockery and cutlery for four persons and large side awning. Exterior colours in choice of either Lotus White, Savanna Beige/White or Brilliant Blue/White.

Standard equipment in the Eurovette comprises:

- Double Bed 6ft 1in by 4ft 6in wide
- Child's cab hammock in Tygan
- Two-burner cooker with grill and oven
- 'Easicool' unit for hygienic food storage
- Cutlery and melamine crockery for four persons
- Drop-leaf table in beauty board
- Fitted sink unit with water pump and 6½-gallon plastic water tank
- Spacious side awning in Royal Blue canvas
- Fluorescent electric lighting run off the vehicle's battery
- Fitted fire extinguisher
- Flooring throughout – relief textured tiles
- Cushions covered in reversible vinyl and Duracour
- Front passenger headrest

⬇ Interior image of the early second-generation Eurovette: while it appears simple today, the interior attributes and quality offered virtually unbounded luxury then.

DANBURY

Danbury Conversions, so named due to their location in the village of the same name, near Chelmsford in Essex, produced their first Campers in 1964, branding the product the Danbury Multicar. However, it was only when George and Joy Dawson joined the firm in 1967 that the operation sprang to prominence and Danbury became one of the three firms to be recognised as Volkswagen official converters. The Danbury sold on price, simplicity and above all, convenience. George Dawson had developed two lockers or base units that could be manoeuvred with ease to act as rearward facing seats at the dining table one minute and forward-facing travelling seats the next. A foldaway cooker grill was stored in one of the base units, while a sink and roof locker more or less completed the package. Danbury sold in excess of 3,000 conversions before Devon obtained exclusive licensing for 1972.

Today inevitably, a Danbury conversion looks rather basic, but a good number have survived and are usually in good condition. Hardly the most luxurious of classic Campers, nevertheless the Danbury based on the second-generation Transporter is a suitable option for concours, or even weekends away.

⬇ Danbury's simple layout altered little throughout the lifespan of the second-generation Transporter.

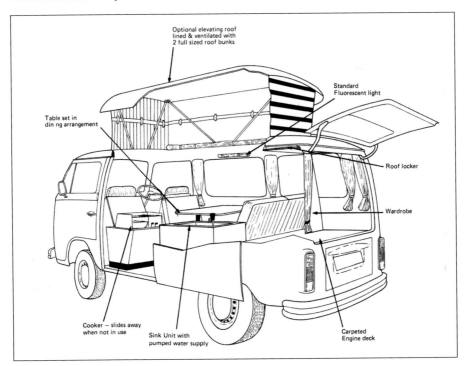

Optional elevating roof lined & ventilated with 2 full sized roof bunks

Standard Fluorescent light

Table set in dining arrangement

Roof locker

Wardrobe

Cooker — slides away when not in use

Sink Unit with pumped water supply

Carpeted Engine deck

EXTRACTS FROM DANBURY'S 1971 BROCHURE

Danbury Conversions take you and your family into 1971 Caravanning with safety, comfort and ease! We can, through our Volkswagen conversion, accommodate the largest of families fully equipped for a carefree "away-from-it-all" holiday, any time of the year, anywhere.

Travel in complete comfort, cook, dine, wash-up easily, and finally set out whatever sleeping accommodation you wish ... quickly and simply – the Danbury way – the 1971 way!

Travelling – The two forward lockers slide back and lock in a forward-facing position (no travel sickness) and all the cushions are deep foam, covered with modern colourful fabrics which are so easily cleaned, and so smart.

Cooking – The Danbury high-pressure cooker (standard on all models) is functional, super-efficient and swings down into the front locker when not in use ... thus creating another seat for that extra traveller.

Dining – You can easily transform the separate front seats into a bench, giving comfortable seats for the whole family.

Clearing Away– After meals, the washing up is easily done in the Danbury full-size sink, which of course has a pumped water supply.

Bed-time– For the adults, double or twin beds in a matter of moments. A child sleeps across the beautifully insulated engine deck (useful point ... much less noise when travelling). A further child's stretcher bunk can be easily fitted across the cab (as an optional extra).

DORMOBILE

Whereas the Devon brand was destined be sold well into the 1980s and eventually more or less drift away from Volkswagen, while Danbury would cease trading towards the end of the decade, the once mighty Dormobile was destined to fall at the end of the 1970s. Conversions on the Transporter were always largely peripheral to the Martin Walter organisation, but a reasonable number of conversions dating from the late 1960s and 1970s survive and are well worth consideration by those eager to own a quality conversion from several decades ago.

Dormobile introduced the unimaginatively titled D4/6 ('Dormobile sleeps four, seats six') as soon as was realistically practical after the launch of the second-generation Transporter. Although a second model, the people-carrying D4/8, was added to the range in 1970, most sales and, hence surviving examples, were made of the D4/6. Unlike Devon and Westfalia, but in common with Danbury, the D4/6 layout and attributes remained more or less the same throughout its production run.

EXTRACTS FROM DORMOBILE'S 1968 BROCHURE

In the country. On the sand. Or just in the sun ...

... You'll be feeling hungry after the drive down – so raise the front passenger seat for the best-designed caravan cooker ever! It's a big twin-burner and grill with a metalwork top, shelf space and enough room around it to cook a real three-course meal in comfort. The long dining table attaches to the cabinet side by the bench seat and the cutlery drawer is right next to it. You'll find two free standing camp chairs stowed in a locker over the engine – so the whole family can relax around the table as dinner is served.

The sturdy glass fibre Dormobile roof opens in seconds to give over eight foot of headroom above the central living area and two 5ft 11in roof bunks fold down from the canopy. If the children are ready for bed – then you can be left in the peace of

your own berth below. There are colourful curtains all round, fluorescent interior lighting and plenty of room to wander about even with your bed made up – a luxurious six foot double which simply folds out flat as you raise the back bench seat. ...

... Just take a look at the cabinet work – it's all golden, wood grained melamine. The wardrobe and storage cupboards and all interior fittings are designed to be attractive and practical. The two 6lb gas bottles, for instance, are concealed within the engine compartment; the sink unit is built into the cabinet work – with an efficient foot-pump which draws all the water you need from concealed 3-gallon containers. And then there is the unique luxury feature of the VW Dormobile – a fully insulated ice box, with over 2 cu.ft. capacity, fitted with a hinged lid and wire storage trays ...

➜ The cover image from Dormobile's brochure of 1970 and thereabouts illustrates their classic Martin Walter elevating roof, but as the company sold them to other converters, such a feature is not a guarantee of the less than inspiringly named D4/6. However, the layout was a good one and included the innovative feature of a cooker in the passenger seat area.

1979–1990
THIRD-GENERATION CAMPERS

The conversion companies chosen to represent the range of third-generation Campers might come as a surprise for, with one blatantly obvious exception, all the names are new. Devon's dismissal might appear harsh, but the truth of the matter is that the field is so wide, only the very best or those with a particular tale to tell triumphed in the selection process. Sorry then to those whose passion is to own an Auto-Sleepers conversion based on the T3 – you will have to wait a generation. Apologies too for excluding Autohomes products in total – many fine examples will be available out there on the market. Nor would it be realistic to include the remarkable Tischer Demountable (a piggyback conversion, attached to a Pick-up), Dehler's sophisticated Profi and Karmann's innovative coach-built Gypsy. All three are excluded on the grounds of their relative obscurity.

To exclude Westfalia's latter-day T3 model, the California, would be unrealistic; Richard Holdsworth deserves his craftsman's place, while Motorhomes International are there by the skin of their teeth, a highly original elevating roof providing the story to repeat.

WESTFALIA

The arrival of the third-generation Transporter was complemented by the debut of a new conversion from Westfalia. The Joker, in reality an evolutionary Berlin, was destined to survive for the best part of ten years, although inevitably changes were made to the initial specification, both with more models and trim upgrades, until finally it was replaced in August 1988 by the California. Careful scrutiny of the outgoing model and its replacement quickly reveals that the name change was little more than a marketing exercise; at its simplest, the new name had more appeal. The centre page spread from the four-side brochure is sufficient to whet the appetite for what had become a truly sophisticated, state-of-the-art conversion.

MOTORHOMES INTERNATIONAL

As Motorhomes International had ceased trading by the mid-1980s, their third-generation conversions should carry the appropriate health warning: rust kills and can seriously damage your bank balance. Motorhomes International's lasting claim to fame is twofold: an innovative elevating roof offering an incredible amount of extra camping space and the most aggressive marketing material

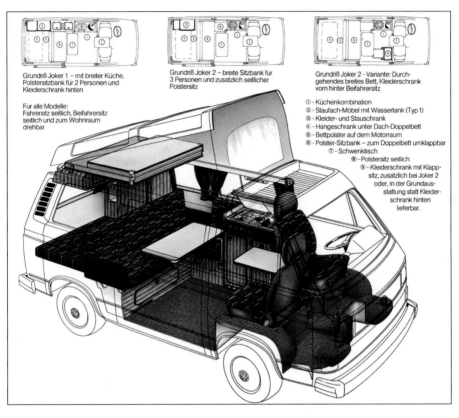

Grundriß Joker 1 – mit breiter Küche, Polstersitzbank für 2 Personen und Kleiderschrank hinten

Für alle Modelle: Fahrersitz seitlich, Beifahrersitz seitlich und zum Wohnraum drehbar

Grundriß Joker 2 – breite Sitzbank für 3 Personen und zusätzlich seitlicher Polstersitz

Grundriß Joker 2 - Variante: Durchgehendes breites Bett, Kleiderschrank vorn hinter Beifahrersitz

① - Küchenkombination
② - Staufach-Möbel mit Wassertank (Typ 1)
③ - Kleider- und Stauschrank
④ - Hangeschrank unter Dach-Doppelbett
⑤ - Bettpolster auf dem Motorraum
⑥ - Polster-Sitzbank – zum Doppelbett umklappbar
⑦ - Schwenktisch
⑧ - Polstersitz seitlich
⑨ - Kleiderschrank mit Klappsitz, zusätzlich bei Joker 2 oder, in der Grundausstattung statt Kleiderschrank hinten lieferbar.

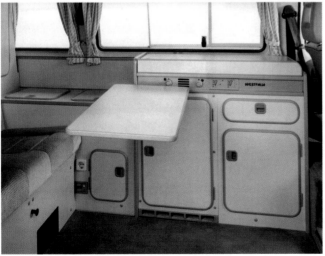

↑ The Westfalia Joker was a revision of the second-generation Transporter layout and one that in turn would be given a makeover to emerge as the California towards the end of the 1980s.

← Centre page spread from a brochure introduced to coincide with the launch of the VW California, in most respects simply an update of the laminates and fabrics used.

SPACEMAKER – A SYSTEM SO FAR ADVANCED AS TO MAKE ALL OTHERS SEEM ALMOST OBSOLETE

We wanted an elevating roof that was semi-automatic, simple and spacious. It had to be full-length to create extra space above the cab for sleeping and storage. This called for an improved lifting mechanism. The traditional coil spring lifting arm couldn't cope. So we used gas-filled arms, pressurised to provide exactly the lifting power we needed for this giant roof. Now, lifting a Spacemaker roof is rather like opening the tailgate of an estate car.

A problem with most elevating roofs is the limited space between bunks. Access is difficult unless the bunks are tapered. To overcome this, the Spacemaker roof is side hinged; so as it opens it overhangs

the side of the van. The side-hinged feature also ensures positive location when the roof is lowered. We then developed an 'overhang' feature along the opposite side. We've created space for both bunks to be moved outwards over the sides of the van - leaving more room to move about inside.

Spacemaker is the most technically advanced elevating roof available anywhere.

We overcame the condensation problem on the glass fibre roof shell by giving it a fabric headlining. And we provide air vents at each end to allow an adequate through current of fresh air. Fly screens ensure that only the air gets in.

imaginable. Naming and attempting to shame their perceived rivals was the order of the day.

The Spacemaker roof system was introduced in 1974 and is seen just as often on a second-generation Transporter as it is in conjunction with the T3. Perhaps potential purchasers might be tempted to locate a second-generation example. (Motorhomes International's sales pitch is reprinted opposite.)

HOLDSWORTH

Richard Holdsworth's involvement with the VW Transporter started more or less when the first-generation models gave way to the Bay and undoubtedly peaked during that vehicle's lifetime and that of its successor, before drifting into receivership in the mid-1990s. A well-preserved Holdsworth Camper based on the second-generation Transporter will undoubtedly be a good investment, but for a level of sophistication previously unheard of, a late-model T3 is the ideal. Holdsworth proved to be a pioneer in the field of offering a fixed high-roof Camper option and, combined with the craftsmanship of his conversions, he was duly showered with accolades during the lifetime of the T3, including the coveted Motor Caravan of the Year title in 1984/85, 1987/88 and 1988/89.

In 1986, the Villa Mk2 was superseded by the Villa Mk3, this being a delightful conversion that was still available when Volkswagen introduced the T4, albeit that Holdsworth had both re-specified and upgraded the model, as was their wont.

Holdsworth's pricelist (reproduced on page 147) and issued at a time when 'like all good things, even the Villa and Vision are coming to an end' (due to the arrival of the fourth-generation Transporter) highlights the wide variety of engine, gearing and additional equipment options available. In theory, such diversity at the time ensures that you should be able to find the ideal Camper of your choice if you search hard enough on the market today.

← Brand new Motorhomes International T3 Campers ready to go. Note the innovative elevating roof design. Out and about, you will see such a roof on later second-generation and earlier T3 models.

⬇ Cover of the final Holdsworth brochure designed to promote the T3-based Villa 3 and Vision, two remarkably fine Campers.

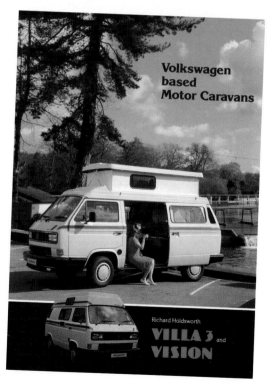

Volkswagen based Motor Caravans

Richard Holdsworth

VILLA 3 and **VISION**

Interior of the Villa 3. Holdsworth's Vision – the Camper with a kitchen at the rear of the vehicle and typical T3 sophistication.

RICHARD HOLDSWORTH VOLKSWAGEN MOTOR CARAVANS SPECIFICATION PRICE LIST, 1 APRIL 1991

The Villas are the only British Volkswagen using genuine German rock and roll bed mechanisms, exclusive slide out tray for changing gas cylinders and 'one action' solid sided elevating roof ... And with the genuine timber used throughout the furniture units plus solid beech cappings, Formica worktops and brass piano hinges, the Villa ... most closely reflect[s] Volkswagen's own legendary quality.

Villa Non Roof Mk 3

Two berth conversion with sliding window caravan section: RM212 Refrigerator/ freezer: Mains input with full safety protection including second battery: Space for toilet: German 'rock and roll' bed mechanism: Swivel cab passenger seat: two rear seat lap restraints: Two burner hob and grill with matching vitreous enamel sink and drainer: Under floor water tank with water level gauge: Upholstered cab seats ...
Based on 1.9 litre petrol engine with five speed gearbox £16,5920.24

Villa Elevating Roof Mk 3

Conversion as above but with 'one action' solid sided elevating roof and including two rear lap restraints and second battery ...
Based on 1.9 litre petrol engine with five speed gearbox £17,678.40

Villa High Top Mk 3

Conversion as above, based on Volkswagen High Roof Van with standing room to cab windscreen ...
Based on 1.9 litre petrol engine with five speed gearbox £17,844.96

Vehicle specification

1.9 litre water cooled petrol engine with servo-assisted brakes, heater and demister, heated rear window, two speed windscreen wipers with intermittent wash/ wipe, trip recorder and clock, dipping rear view mirror, door tray, padded steering wheel, Carat bumpers, double rectangular grill, wheel caps, illuminated passenger mirror, tool kit and inertia seat belts, spare wheel and rear wash/wipe.

Optional equipment

Based on 1.7 diesel 57bhp/ 5 speed gearbox	£1,053.62
Based on 1.6 diesel turbo charged engine 5 speed gearbox	£1,723.55
Automatic transmission on 78bhp	£831.55
Based on 2.1 FI petrol engine 112bhp/5 speed gearbox	£1,051.15
Based on 2.1 FI petrol engine 112bhp/automatic	£1,547.12
Based on 2.1 FI catalytic petrol engine 92bhp	£1,632.25
Based on syncro 4 wheel drive turbo diesel, 70bhp	£6,831.27
Swivel cab driver's seat and cab table £80 & £40	£148.05
Solid roof bed – elevating roof model	£98.70
Solid roof bed – high top roof model	£159.15
Flyscreens for sliding window	£45.65
Flyscreens for high top windows	£53.05
Cab headrests (pair)	£61.69
Storage shelf in cab of high roof	£76.49
Blown air central heating thermostatically controlled	£425.64

1990–2003
FOURTH-GENERATION CAMPERS

The variety of fourth-generation luxury Campers available is truly amazing. One of the key determining factors has to be the relocation of the engine to the front of the vehicle and Volkswagen's resultant ability to offer a chassis-cab option. This proved a real boon to the conversion companies wishing to offer a spacious coach-built motorhome, rather than simply offering the traditional, and more restricted, layout of units within the confines of the van body shell.

Devon and others here in the UK had offered budget conversions for many years, each of which might aptly be referred to as weekenders rather than fully fledged Campers. Similarly, during the lifetime of the T3, Volkswagen started to experiment with its own multi-purpose option, or Multivan, but it was only with the debut of the T4 that such a vehicle became a part of the official line-up. Perhaps inevitably, despite strong sales and a vibrant Camper market, due to its right-hand-drive status, the UK market was one of the last to be allowed a Multivan as part of the standard range. Nevertheless, it appears logical to concentrate here on this vehicle and the 'motorhome', safe in the knowledge that anyone wanting a traditional Camper will have no difficulty in tracking down a wide variety of options from an equally extensive field of converters.

AUTO-SLEEPERS

Cotswold-based Auto-Sleepers has origins dating back to 1961, but it wasn't until the 1980s that its Volkswagen-based business became significant. Those eager to purchase an Auto-Sleepers conversion based on the T3 might find earlier models referred to by a combination of letters and numbers such as VT20, VHT, or VX50. Fortunately, towards the end of the T3's production run, the conversions had been given names. The Trooper was the version with an elevating roof, while the option with a fixed 'Hi-Top' (more Auto-Sleepers terminology) was the Trident.

➜ Auto-Sleepers engaged an advertising agency who generated lifestyle imagery guaranteed to enhance the desirability of already highly attractive Monocoque conversions.

From a range produced around the time that the long-nose version of the T4 (and the VR6 petrol plus 2.5TDI engines) emerged, encompassing seven options, the final conversions in November 2003 had been slimmed down to three. To clarify, where once there had been the Trooper (elevating roof), Trident and Topaz (fixed high tops) and four motorhomes (Clubman, Gatcombe, Sherbourne and Medallion), there remained the Topaz LE, Clubman Anniversary LE and Gatcombe LE.

AUTO-SLEEPERS MONOCOQUE

The renowned Auto-Sleepers Monocoque is a one-piece, aerodynamically designed glassfibre body that is stylish and practical. The unitary construction ensures there are no seams to leak and Monocoques are extremely robust – the perfect partner to the VW Transporter chassis ...

Dimensions – Clubman/Gatcombe
(standard van with high roof in brackets)
Length: 5525mm (5202mm)
Body width (mirrors folded) 2170mm
(1940mm)
Height (without aerial) 2725mm (2555mm)
Double Bed 1905 x 1350mm
(1780 x 1475mm)
Single Bed (offside) 1850 x 680mm
(1780 x 560mm)
Single Bed (nearside) 1870 x 710mm
(1854 x 560mm)

■ One piece unitary construction ensures the Monocoque is extremely robust and there are no seams to leak
■ Manufactured in colour impregnated gelcoat, it is easily maintained
■ Reinforced bonded fittings are included for cycle racks and awnings
■ Fire resistant gelcoat is used in the manufacture of the glassfibre coachwork
■ High levels of insulation including a bonded construction floor and double glazed windows are standard
■ The roof is reinforced for the fitting of top boxes. Moulded tread pads are incorporated into the roof for safety
■ The caravan door lock assembly is burst proof

← The Auto-Sleeper
Gatcombe LE.

Topaz LE daytime

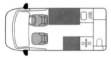

Topaz LE night-time

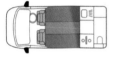

Gatcombe LE daytime

Gatcombe LE night-time

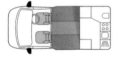

Clubman Anniversary LE daytime

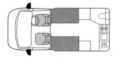

Clubman Anniversary LE night-time

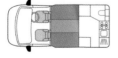

← The Topaz – 'The neat fully equipped shower and toilet compartment has clever space-saving sliding doors – but if you don't want to bring the outdoors inside ... you can enter the washroom through the tailgate!'

← The Gatcombe and the kitchen you can't see! 'The smart rear kitchen is supplied with everything required to turn out a romantic dinner for two, or a big family Sunday lunch, with a four-burner hob/grill and oven next to a stainless steel sink and drainer. A 70-litre fridge and bespoke drinks cabinet are housed in an adjacent unit.'

← 'If you're touring in the Clubman Anniversary LE, you're touring with style and peace of mind.'

CLUBMAN ANNIVERSARY LE CONVERSION FEATURES NOVEMBER 2003

- Aerodynamically designed glassfibre Monocoque coachwork
- Stainless steel roof rack and ladder
- Rear corner steadies
- Centre dinette with choice of two tables (option of small or large pedestal tables or both)
- Two longitudinal single beds or one large double
- Traditional style cabinet work with hardwood edging
- Wood effect fascia trim
- Under-floor storage locker
- Storage available in large over-cab locker
- Cab seats in matching upholstery
- High quality reflex foam upholstery
- Scatter cushions
- Removable bound edged carpet on vinyl floor
- Lined curtains
- Four-burner hob with grill and oven each with electronic ignition
- Stainless steel sink and drainer with dual purpose glass lid that can be used either as a chopping board or as an extra work surface
- 70lt refrigerator powered by gas/12v/230v with freezer compartment and electronic ignition
- Crockery for four in dedicated storage unit
- Truma thermostatically controlled space heater with 230v Ultraheat blown air-heating system.
- Truma Ultrastore gas/230v water heater supplies sink, shower and hand-basin
- Shower with chrome mixer tap, full width cassette toilet, vanity unit, glass mirror, towel rail, large hand-basin and non-slip shower mat, roof skylight with fly-screen and double glazed opaque acrylic window
- Combined overhead lighting is provided by fluorescent lights and halogen reading lights where fitted
- Double glazed windows in the living area with cassette blinds and fly-screens
- Heki roof ventilator with night blind and fly-screen
- Roof ventilator with blind and fly-screen
- Electrical control panel incorporates a water level indicator, master switches for 12v lighting and water pump, with individual trip switches for each circuit
- Mains electric input with safety trip switch (earth leakage circuit breaker)
- Mains charging system for vehicle and secondary battery with 12v split charge relay
- Three 230v socket and one 12v socket
- Bespoke television cabinet with pull-out turntable
- Combined TV aerial and booster
- 69lt fresh water tank and 67lt waste water tank
- External locker for two 7kg gas cylinders
- Smoke alarm and fire extinguisher
- Automotive style anti-burst caravan door lock
- Removable step

Standard Automotive Specification
- Engine - 2.5 TDI diesel, output 102bhp

Conversion options
- Front forward facing seat, in lieu of inward facing dinette seat on offside with inertia reel seatbelt converts into inward facing settee
- Extractor fan in lieu of roof ventilator
- Pull out over-cab bed in place of storage locker
- Optional upholstery available
- Waste bin on caravan door
- Refrigerator with full width freezer compartment

THE MULTIVAN

A fair number of left-hand-drive Multivans are available on the market, but right-hand-drive examples are a rare commodity, as the vehicle only became part of the UK range in 1997. Find a short-nose Multivan and it won't have been sold originally in a UK showroom, and for that matter, come across a special-edition long-nose Multivan, of which there are quite a few, and that will have its steering wheel on the 'wrong' side.

With a degree of inevitability, when the Multivan finally made it to way across the English Channel, the UK Press office was quick to point out that it was a Caravelle- rather than Transporter-based product and such was the degree of luxury afforded to it that it carried the equivalent of GL, or virtual top-of-the-range trim levels. Initially offered with either the sloth-like 2.4SD in automatic guise, or the altogether more dynamic 2.5TDI power plant, once into the new millennium the options had been extended to include first the 114PS and later 140PS V6 petrol engines, as well as an 88PS TDI oil burner.

Compared to say, for example, German market Multivans, the UK offer was always more restricted. By the 2000 model year, German Multivans were offered with three different levels of trim: basic, Trendline and Comfortline. An under-seat cool-box was included as standard equipment, while there was also an option to include an elevating roof. Best of all for the favoured few, a syncro Multivan was much more than an enthusiast's pipe dream.

➜ The imagery in most of Volkswagen's brochures covering the T4 Multivan emphasised its practical nature as a day or weekend-away vehicle. Here from the home-market brochure dating from 2002, the Multivan is seen as an ideal base for a picnic (this page), or simply somewhere to relax (with the rear seats collapsed to bed mode (page opposite).

MULTIVAN UK MARKET SPECIFICATION (2002 MODEL YEAR)

- ABS with Electronic Differential Lock (V6 only)
- Body-coloured door mirrors, body-coloured foam-filled bumpers
- Central locking
- Driver's airbag (V6 only)
- Driver's seat adjustable for lumber support, reach and take
- Heated and adjustable door mirrors
- Folding rear seat row – folds back for use as a bed
- Folding table located on offside rear compartment wall
- Head restraints, height adjustable
- Lowered suspension
- Map light for front seat passengers
- Passenger seat adjustable for reach and rake
- Rear luggage platform cover with additional cover for bed
- Sliding window above table
- Snap on and off window curtains
- Two rear-facing, removable seats with tip-up seat bases
- Trim – Grey 'Toto' cloth (also offered on the Caravelle Sedan, but not on the more upmarket Variant or Limousine models)

2003–2015
FIFTH-GENERATION CAMPERS

Predictability concurrent with 21st-century lifestyles, a wealth of Camper conversion companies offered more and more sophisticated and luxurious layouts for Volkswagen's much-loved fifth-generation Transporter. Despite the retro appeal of the second- and particularly the first-generation Camper conversions, the basic nature and limited practicality of a vehicle that could easily be 50 years old remained questionable in the eyes of many would-be owners. The trend towards gadgetry and opulence, which had become evident in the 1980s, part-way through the production run of the T3, gathered pace during the lifetime of the T4, just as it would over the decade and more of T5 activity at Hanover.

⬇ California on the move. Kitchen unit. Ready to dine.

VOLKSWAGEN PRESS AND PUBLIC RELATIONS – CALIFORNIA SE 2.5 LITRE TDI 174PS – 2006 – TEST VEHICLE SPECIFICATION

Performance:

Engine capacity (litres/cc): 2.5/2,460

Power output (PS @rpm): 174 @ 3,500

Maximum torque (Nm @ rpm): 400/2,000

Top speed (mph): 115

0–62 mph (seconds): 13.0

Fuel economy (mpg): Urban 25.7, Extra urban 41.5, Combined 34.0

Fuel tank capacity (litres): 80

Service intervals (miles): Longlife (variable) service regime

Warranty: Three years or 100,000 miles, twelve-year body protection

Colour and Trim:

Raven Blue with Scala Grey/Blue art Grey cloth upholstery

Upgrade to 'Climatronic' air conditioning, alloy wheels 'Solace' 17in with 235/55 R17 tyres, satellite navigation – colour screen with trip computer

Standard features include:

ABS with EDL (Electronic Differential Lock) and ASR (traction control), ESP (Electronic Stabilisation Programme)

Driver and front-passenger airbags – front, side and curtain (front passenger airbag de-activation with vehicle key)

Remote central locking, with deadlocking and internal locking button, alarm, includes interior and tow-away protection

Electric front windows, electrically heated, adjustable and folding body-coloured exterior mirrors

Heated front seats, driver and passenger swivelling seats with lumbar support, reach and rake adjustment, with armrests

Two folding chairs (stored in tailgate), folding table, clothes cupboard and storage compartments, blackout blinds, draw curtains for side windows

Gas cooker, two burners, burner power approx 1000W/1800W, power from 2.8kg gas cylinder (not supplied), energy consumption rated approx 140g/hr, safety tank valve, gas pressure regulator, shut-off valve for gas feed

Cooler Waeco, 42-litre capacity, cooling system compression unit

Kitchen cabinet, sink/cooler combination with height-adjustable safety cover, stainless steel sink with single tap (with switch for water pump) storage compartments

Roof bed (120 x 200cm) with gas-spring supported pivoting mechanism, ventilation windows, insertable child safety net, gooseneck halogen lamp

Fresh water container (30 litres), waste water tank (30 litres), protected against freezing in passenger compartment

Pop-up aluminium roof (electro-hydraulically activated) with two attachment rails for roof rack system

Bench/bed – reclining bench seat with backrest adjustable to three positions, fully reclined with headrests folded back and the backrest released, forms a 114 x 200cm bed

Heating and fresh-air system with manual air conditioning, dust and pollen filter, parking heater with radio remote control

THE CROMFORD, ONE OF SEVERAL OPTIONS OFFERED ON THE T5 TRANSPORTER BY HILLSIDE LEISURE

Based on the long-wheelbase Volkswagen Transporter, with the choice of an elevating roof or factory high top.

Flexible internal layout:
Daytime: On the road – four single, forward-facing seats. When parked – the two front seats spin rearwards to create a seating area. Alternatively, the driver's seat reclines and, with two inward facing seats, makes a sofa along the side of the vehicle.
Night-time: The seats make two single beds or one large king-size bed. A large double bed is formed in the roof space. Behind the rear seats is a galley-style kitchen. A three-ring hob, grill, oven and storage occupies one side, while opposite there is a sink with 50ltr fridge underneath. Also on this side is a sliding shelve unit with door that cloaks off the rear bathroom. The bathroom itself incorporates a cassette toilet, drop down vanity sink, wardrobe and a selection of storage cupboards

- Weaco 50ltr low-energy fridge with ice box
- Waste tank under slung so as not to take up internal space
- Vanity sink
- Sink with integrated tap
- Low-energy LED lights
- Leisure battery with split-charging system
- Fresh water tank under-slung so not to take up internal space
- Eberspächer diesel blown-air heating
- Combined grill and oven
- Cassette toilet
- Both front seats swivel
- Activity shower
- 240-volt hot-water heating system
- 240-volt fuse box with trip switches

➜ Rapid transformation to a comfortable double bed.

However, there was one enormous difference with regard to the T5. For the first time in 53 years or thereabouts, Volkswagen had little option but to offer a Camper in their showrooms, a product of their own workforce under the auspices of the VWCV Special Business Unit. Westfalia had become a property of Volkswagen's rivals. In 1999, the formidable Daimler-Chrysler-Mercedes-Benz group had acquired a 49 per cent stake in Westfalia's conversion division. By 2001 they were well on the way to absorbing the remaining 51 per cent. Although Westfalia continued to build conversions based on the T4, they were clearly disqualified as recipients of prototypes of the next-generation Transporter. In 2004, the first VW factory manufactured Campers emerged into the sunlight. The coup-de-grâce as far as Westfalia were concerned came when Volkswagen's T5 Camper was named the California.

By way of comparison, and possibly helping to illustrate the relatively simple nature of the VW California conversion, opposite is an edited version of a new-wave and relatively small-scale converter's description and specification highlights. Clearly, in T5 times it was a case of make your choice and assess value for money.

↑ With the roof raised an airy room in which to relax.

CHAPTER 5
CUSTOMISING
YOUR CAMPER

Of all the chapters, this is probably the most difficult to write. Why? Because the whole point of customising is to create something individual, an expression of personal taste. There isn't a convenient array of brochures to dive into with which to educate stock devotees. Nor can potential owners of later model customised vehicles be given directions to showrooms across the country conveniently full of such Transporters ready to floor and hurtle homewards. Unless you are talking T5, there isn't even a Camper conversion company that lowers, repaints and adds the wilder of wheels as part of one of their standard specification vans. You are on your own, but, budgets allowing, isn't that also part of the fun of customising?

Fortunately though, for the aesthetically challenged there are trends in customising that extend to all generations (both of vehicles and owners). Lowering is a favoured one (although some ground-hug and others don't), creating a rat look is another (and one worthy by its controversial nature of at least a paragraph or two elsewhere), deliberately aging the vehicle is a third (there's a pattern to the patina of customised vehicles). Devotees of sign writing err towards the older Campers (and if truth is told, more to commercials, such as the Delivery Van and Pick-up). Those who deliberately buff and polish away the paint again tend to select the older vehicles, but in this instance a Camper is definitely fair game. Those adding vinyl (the modern way to decorate any vehicle, from an Eddie Stobart articulated lorry to a local white van man declaring his trade) – from a complete panel wrap to such simple adornments as stripes or bands – may well opt to do this to a T3 or later generation Camper.

As far as the engine of a customised vehicle goes, casual observation suggests greater cubic capacity (than stock). Additions appear essential, either aesthetic (for which read chrome and paint) or power boosting (the desired effect being more PS or BHP). One other option is yanking an engine out of a vehicle bearing the badge of another manufacturer and crowbarring it into whichever generation of Transporter is preferred.

Suspension work and (on earlier models) the addition of disc brakes seem the norm, as does a meaty exhaust. Few, if any, customised vehicles run on standard wheels – indeed, many largely stock Campers are shod with special wheels and that's just as true of many recent T5s as it is of 1960s first-generation models.

Drifting in the direction of paint once more, the customised Transporter devotee literally has a blank canvas. Do you include the 'original is best' man who decides he simply can't live with Volkswagen's chosen paint shade for the vehicle and opts therefore to have it resprayed in a colour correct for the year but not the Camper? The answer is probably not, for this is a field where not only decades may separate the Camper's year of manufacture and the chosen VW shade but also a world of modern gentle pearlescent paints and the more radical gamut of every conceivable manufacturer's colour chart for as many years of their existence as deemed necessary.

Once inside the vehicle though, you are definitely more or less on your own. The interior of a customised Camper, whether mild or wild, is personal. Some may opt to acquire original furniture from years gone by, while others might decide to copy particular gems from the past. Immediately, Devon's curved cabinet springs to mind as an example and must have done so for quite a few owners too, judging by the number of beautifully rounded pieces of Camper furniture seen at the shows. With drapes, a scattering of cushions and a personal choice of floor covering that could well be it for many, but for others the music studio beckons, the state-of-the-art outdoor kitchen calls, the fashionable Southwold beach hut look prevails and the surfboard story is to be played out.

The customised Camper devotee has a choice. Either he or she buys a ready-made customised model and in the process loses half the fun of designing what hits the spot, or the search is on for a sound shell on which to work their own particular kind of magic. Whichever it is, perhaps it would be helpful to read about the basics of what others have done before to older Transporters.

The interior of a customised Camper, whether mild or wild, is personal. Some may opt to acquire original furniture from years gone by, while others might decide to copy particular gems from the past.

FOUR CUSTOMISED EXAMPLES
FIRST-GENERATION CAMPERS

DOUBLE-DOOR CAMPER

Originally a Delivery Van with twin side loading doors

- Repainted many years ago white over blue and Microbus De Luxe trim added. Paint has faded or been bleached by the sun giving sought-after patina
- Roof rack and side ladder added
- Safari windows
- 1,641cc engine, twin Kadron carbs, 009 dizzy, flamethrower coil, alternator conversion, Empi fat boy exhaust and manifold
- KYB lowered gas shocks, spline removed at the rear
- Folksy adjuster on rebuilt front beam
- BRM wheels – 4.5 front, 5.5 rear – Bridgestone Potenza tyres 165/55/15 front and 185/55/15 rear
- Interior created out of marine ply and covered in paint matching blur vinyl with white piping
- Upper panels and headlining in mohair
- Cab seats retrimmed to match rear
- Custom billet steering wheel

1963 13-WINDOW MICROBUS DE LUXE

- Beige Grey over Porsche Kelly Green
- Pop-out windows all round
- Lowered by six inches, gas shocks at front end, otherwise stock, rear Volksheaven IRS conversion on Type 3 gearbox
- Empi five spokes
- 1,835cc engine, stock heads and valves – bolt together rocker gear with swivel feet adjusters, chrome molly push rods, 92mm barrels and pistons, stock stroked, welded and finned counterweighted crank, lightened flywheel, Engle 110 cam with aluminium drive gear, AS41 crank case, high-flow oil pump, twin 40 Webers, Pierburg electric fuel pump, electronic ignition, flamethrower coil
- Main storage unit against front bulkhead, with lift-up section revealing cooker and underneath lift-out cool-box
- Roof cabinet at rear for additional storage
- New cloth headliner
- Side panels and seats trimmed in pale green vinyl with Westfalia-style check inserts
- Surfboard style fold-down table
- Child's cab bed
- Extra cushions for double bed stored in rear luggage area

1965 KOMBI

- Bare metal respray pearlescent Kandy Apple Red (over Orion Silver base) roof and lower panels with Old English White centre section
- Front and rear safari windows
- Chromed pop-outs
- Polished stainless-steel bumpers
- Clear rear light lenses
- Creative 'Weedeater' adjustable beam, Creative IRS with adjustable spring plates
- Creative Dropped Spindles, CSP disc brakes, new rear hubs
- Fully chromed replica Fuchs alloys
- 1,776cc engine – new crankcase and heads, Engle 110 cam, Mahle barrels and pistons, new valves, HD Melling oil pump, double thrust cam bearings, high carbon push rods, HD swivel feet adjusters, Bosch alternator and 009 dizzy, reground forged crank, new shell bearings. Twin Webber 40s, stainless-steel quiet pack exhaust.
- Powder coated Old English White engine tinware
- Full-width rock and roll bed
- Full-width storage unit with curved end in walnut burr laminate with dark-wood edging across bulkhead with matching roof cupboard
- Cream vinyl upholstery with contrasting quilted red Alcantara fabric
- Banjo steering wheel, scat shifter

1956 WOLFSBURG KOMBI BECOMES A CAMPER FOR TWO

- Panel replacement and bare metal respray in VW Mineral Grey Metallic over BMW Phoenix Yellow
- Tinted side window glass
- Chromed side bars attached to sills, chromed indicator bullet housings, Samba chromed front badge and chromed period klaxon
- Chromed front and rear Safari windows, chromed 'split screen' script badge below the rear tailgate
- Full-length, Westfalia-style roof rack
- Interior units built from sanded ply sealed with Danish Oil
- Full width bench/bed facing full width bulkhead seat
- Interior, including side panels and door cards, upholstered in a combination of grey leather and contrasting Alcantara panels
- Reversible seat cushions with one side finished in grey crushed Dralon
- Roof lined with ply
- Drop-down silk drapes
- Billet 56 Steering wheel
- Diesel heater
- Drop-down TV/DVD
- Folding hob/grill located on rear side loading door, supported by plywood board when in use
- Street rod stance – IRS conversion, adjustable spring plates, dropped spindle, narrowed front beam and CSP disc conversion
- Creative Engineering steering rack
- 1500 engine block bored and fitted with 1641cc pistons, twin Webber carbs, electronic ignition

None of the Campers photographed on these two page can really be described as extreme examples of the art of customising a Volkswagen. Essentially, the vehicle illustrated top left is a straightforward Westfalia SO42 that has been repainted in a bright body colour and adorned with floral-pattern curtains. Similarly, the apparently standard colours carried by the Samba (bottom left) are enhanced by accessories such as a roof rack, headlamp protectors, chromed bumpers and alloys. In a similar vein, the VW Camper top right sports accessories, but has also been lowered. The rarity of the conversion depicted middle right will be overlooked by some drawn to its flowery decals. The final image of a strikingly stock SO42 Camper (bottom right), slammed to within an inch of its life for showing purposes, illustrates how anything goes in the world of customising.

FOUR CUSTOMISED EXAMPLES
SECOND-GENERATION CAMPERS

1970 WESTFALIA SO67 – COMBINING STREET CREDIBILITY WITH ORIGINAL INTERIOR AND EXTERNAL PATINA

- Repainted pop top and bumpers, all other paintwork buffed, front panel deliberately left stone-chipped
- Original SO67 interior, with Eberspächer D2 diesel heater
- Empi shifter, dash-mounted tachometer and under-dash oil temperature, pressure and amp gauges
- Wagens West 4in narrowed adjustable beam
- Bustang disc brakes and 2½in drop spindles
- Adjustable spring plates at the rear
- Flat 4 Sprintstars on 175/55 15 tyres at the front and 185/65/15 at the rear
- 1,904cc engine – case bored for 92mm, drilled for full flow oil, 74mm balanced crankshaft, lightweight 8-dowelled flywheel, 30mm heavy-duty oil pump, Mahle forged pistons, Twin Weber 40s
- Engine mated to a late Bay 6-rib gearbox with higher ratio 4th gear for motorway cruising

SUBARU SAN CAMPMOBILE

- Original colour combination of Dakota Beige under Pastel White roof panel
- Chrome front badge and smoked indicator housings
- Wood rim stainless steel steering wheel, Wolfsburg-badged window winders
- Empi shifter, polished ally handbrake, dash-mounted rev counter and temperature gauge
- Centreline alloys
- Refurbished original style Westfalia Berlin interior
- 2.2-litre, 16-valve Subaru engine offering 145bhp
- Savage exhaust and gauges
- Additional cooling/air circulation vents let into engine lid behind number plate, which now stands proud to maximise flow
- Racing disc brakes

1975 LHD BAY DELIVERY VAN BECOMES A CAMPER

- Resprayed Tornado Red under Pastel White roof panel with colour-coded bumpers
- Chrome headlight eyelids, matching red sun visor, whitewall tyres and baby moon hubcaps
- Devon-style pop-top, louvered window above/behind kitchen unit, roof rack over cab
- 1,641cc colour-coded 'green' engine, single Weber carb, sports air filter, Bug Pack exhaust
- Lowered by 100mm
- Main kitchen unit, including sink, hob and fridge aligned to sit opposite side loading door.
- ¾ rock and roll bed to rear, with slender storage unit following kitchen unit.
- Units finished in light oak with walnut tops, door and drawer fronts finished in high gloss red (to match exterior paint colour)
- Rear bench seat, buddy seat, spare-wheel cover and rear cushion upholstered in cream leatherette with button finish
- Red and white check curtains. Side panels and roof foam lined and covered in matching cream vinyl – extended to cab door panels
- Chromed LED spot lights
- Replica 1970s bucket seats in the cab, black with red piping

1970 DANBURY

(Aqua Blue under Cloud White Danbury in need of restoration)

- Front panel, arches, rear corners, sills and cab doors replaced
- Bare metal respray in Porsche metallic Tahoe Blue with VW Arctic White roof panel and bumpers
- MCJ steering wheel, oil pressure and temperature gauges, rev counter, satellite navigation
- Porsche black leather cab seats
- Danbury interior copied (wardrobe and overhead locker not replaced) and produced in a combination of white units and black with white piping seats and cushions. Blue and white matching curtains and ties
- Ivory White headlining
- Fully adjustable front beam narrowed by two inches – drop spindles and coil-over shocks
- Rear – two spline drop, adjustable spring plates and Gaz shocks
- 15in chrome Fuchs
- 1,776cc engine, twin Emp 40s, Engle 110 cam, CB performance 044 twin port heads mated to ceramic turbo muffler exhaust, alternator, Petronix electronic ignition
- Engine bay and engine fully detailed to match exterior

Without doubt, paint and colour co-ordination is the major theme of these four Campers. Note specifically how those vehicles with their side-loading doors open illustrate the level of care taken to match the inside to the exterior. The zenith in such a process though has to be the delightful canvas roof of the lime green Camper.

FOUR CUSTOMISED EXAMPLES
THIRD-GENERATION CAMPERS

MAKEOVER FOR A 1980 DEVON MOONRAKER T3 CAMPER

- Original colour scheme of burgundy under cream exterior retained and interior colour coded to match. Unit doors finished in burgundy and aluminium handles fitted. Interior carpets replaced with dark grey pattern, which is burgundy edged. Marble effect flooring fitted
- Original dated brown Dralon upholstery replaced with burgundy vinyl, edged with cream piping. Extended to panels, curtains and scatter cushions made out of period style plaid fabric
- Interior upgrades include a diesel Eberspächer heater, flip-down TV/DVD, cab captain's chairs and Caravelle steering wheel
- 1.6 air-cooled engine replaced with 2.0-litre version mated to appropriate gearbox. Twin 40 Dellorto carbs fitted
- Turbo Thomas stainless-steel exhaust and J tubes
- Lowered by 45mm using H&R kit, new steel wheels with 'baby-moon' hubcaps

BUILDER'S VAN TO COOL CAMPER

1987 Delivery Van with 2.0-litre engine finished in Pastel White

- Side windows cut into panels – half smoked glass
- Resprayed in Nissan (Figaro) Lapis Grey
- Smoked front indicator lenses and rear light clusters
- Front visor
- Quarter-size roof rack and Fiamma bike rack
- Cab seats reupholstered in cream vinyl with pale grey piping
- Custom built units in light oak veneer with fridge, cooker, grill, sink and water tank.
- Pale grey carpets with lighter shade of grey binding
- Rock 'n' roll bed
- Lowered by 40mm
- 18in Audi S4 wheels with Continental 245/45 tyres
- Weber carb

1982 2.0-LITRE DELIVERY VAN

(Originally Burgundy Red, rebuilt original air-cooled engine)

- Sliding side door replaced with twin cargo doors
- Windows let into fabricated cargo doors
- Standard VW sliding window let in opposite cargo doors
- One piece cab door windows
- All glass except windscreen tinted
- GRP Body Kit
- South African style front grille and modified grille spoiler
- Smoked indicator lenses
- Body de-seamed and resprayed in VW Sari Yellow
- 18in Demon Tweaks wheels
- Fabricated roof rack and ladder painted VW Sari Yellow
- Peugeot cab seats with swivel base
- Fully demountable cooker, including grill, hob and oven
- Under-floor storage area – hole cut in floor and box fabricated between the chassis
- Side and roof panels lined with fake fur animal fabrics

CARAVELLE TO SUBARU SYNCRO

(Originally a 1986 Caravelle syncro with 14in wheels, 2.1-litre petrol engine)

- Respray in Mercedes Ice Blue
- Full pop-top Westfalia roof
- Sound deadening, insulation and flooring fitted
- Original blue door cards and seats re-trimmed in grey throughout
- ¾ rock 'n' roll seat/bed
- Light oak veneer and light blue Formica chosen for Camper units, which are positioned on the opposite side to the side-loading door
- No wardrobe to block visibility. Electrolux three-way fridge, Smev sink and Smev two burner hob, two drawers under the grill and space for a 20-litre water container (with submersible pump), 4.5kg gas bottle
- Overhead locker in the style of Westfalia originals
- Two tables – small one fitted to passenger seat base
- Uprated lift springs and OME shocks
- Modified rear trailing arms for 16in wheels and tyres
- 16in syncro wheel-arch trims, syncro truck mirrors, rear wheel carrier
- 16in Granada Cosworth Scorpio wheels – 225/75/16 Goodyear Wrangler tyres
- 2.5 DOHC normally aspirated Subaru engine (from a Legacy Outback), rebuilt to include turbo clutch bell housing, full stainless-steel exhaust, Burley shortened sump

To the left, three examples of the particularly popular cult of deliberately aging the patina of the vehicle, but don't be fooled – the sign-writing isn't original and the paint finishes weren't applied in the year of the vehicle's manufacture. The vehicle at the top is the probable exception as here original paint appears to have been polished and polished and polished to give an aged look.

Two variations on a theme for the T4 Camper: above – a radical colour scheme ensures 21st-century relevance and below – the craft of accentuating features to create a unique look.

FOUR CUSTOMISED EXAMPLES
FOURTH-GENERATION CAMPERS

FROM 2.4TDI KOMBI VAN TO FULLY FLEDGED CAMPER:

- Side and rear windows blacked out, stainless-steel sidebars, colour-coded bumpers and wing mirrors, chromed handles
- LED rear lights, front lights black Audi style
- Plain black bonnet bra
- Lowered to 60mm clearance, 18in Borbet two-tone alloys, heavy-duty springs.
- Powerflow exhaust with split tailpipe, separate silencers and back boxes.
- MDF units finished in lacquered light cream, kitchen unit along the driver's side, built in fridge/freezer, built in SMEV gas hob and sink with black glass top.
- ¾ rock 'n' roll bed, black venetian blinds on the side windows, full cab and rear window blackout curtains
- Six roof lining mounted spotlights and roof-mounted, drop-down TV/ DVD player
- Black and cream carpets over dark wood effect vinyl, door cards covered in black acoustic carpet, door pockets finished in cream stitched vinyl, chromed handles and window winders
- Captain seats reupholstered in black and cream vinyl with stitched VW logo on back panel
- Coloured dashboard

FROM 1993 CARAVELLE TO CAMPER

(Caravelle with central locking, electric windows, electric mirrors, sliding centre side windows and 2.4 diesel engine, finished in Metallic Burgundy)

- Resprayed in Audi Metallic InkaGelb over Pearl Orange
- Full body-kit fitted – front and rear bumpers, side skirts and wheel arches
- Lowered by 60mm
- Audi A8 18in Alloys 225/45 with VW logo centre caps
- Propex gas controlled heating
- Rear wardrobe, storage and cupboard space built into side unit facing the side sliding door finished in silver/dark grey (harmonising with the side panels and dash)
- ¾ rock 'n' roll bed/rear seat upholstered in silver grey/dark grey and orange piping
- Cab seat bases, curtain ties, speaker grills, heater outlet, handbrake lever colour coded orange
- Captain's seats fitted, passenger seat swivels
- Momo grey steering wheel, fitted grey carpets
- Flip-down 8in TV/DVD

FROM 1.9TD WINDOW VAN TO CAMPER

- Originally Indian Blue, dents and scratches removed and resprayed both inside and outside in BMW Estoril Blue. Bumpers and side mirrors colour-coded
- Lowered by 45mm, Mercedes AMG A-line alloys, load rated tyres and VW centre caps
- De-badged, colour-coded side headlamp eyebrows, clear indicator lenses, marine-grade stainless-steel side bars fitted to sill line. Rear wipers removed, spoilers fixed to rear door tops, clear LED lights. Stainless steel check-plate fitted to rear step
- Side and rear door windows given dark tint, windscreen light smoke
- RVTEC interior in light woodgrain finish. Units on sidewall, smoked glass top Smev hob and sink units, Waeco fridge, wardrobe and storage
- ¾ rear seat finished in blue, with button effect and square panels created by stitching. Also rearward facing seat accessed when doors open. Collapsed, both form the Camper's bed
- Raceline bucket seats in cab, passenger swivel, finished in matching blue upholstery
- Whole interior fully insulated and black thick pile carpeted
- TV/DVD swivel mounted behind the driver's seat

2000 2.5TDI 88PS DELIVERY VAN TO 2-BERTH CAMPER

- Dual side-windows fitted both sides, twin sunroofs added to roof-panel
- Front bumper smoothed (tow hook removed), rear bumper smoothed
- Complete respray retaining Grauss White lower panels under black, the latter being coated with prismatic metal flake. Pinstripe design applied to the rear doors, the vehicle's swage line and the bonnet. Chequerboard detailing added to the front bumper
- Red/clear crystal rear lights, crystal clear front indicators and black metal flake covers for the headlights
- Stainless-steel twin-exit silencer
- Lowered via modified bump-stops, Bilstein B6 shock absorbers and revised rear springs
- Chromed 17in Fuchs replica wheels
- Customised trim plastics, headlining and floor system (thermo acoustic installation upgrades the Transporter to factory Caravelle interior)
- Knobs, handles and window winders finished in purple anodised aluminium and polished alloy
- Variotech full-width, multi-position bed/seat unit – reupholstered, using grey vinyl and check from a T5 Multivan
- Slimline Reimo units housing sink and foldaway hob
- Passenger cab seat replaced with captain's swivelling chair
- Swivel interior lights and LEDs set into cups in the headlining, door handles, door pockets and under the dashboard

At first glance, each of the interiors presented on these pages might have been added to the vehicle by a converter shortly after it was manufactured. However, all are recent bespoke craftsman additions. The furniture depicted top and bottom left pays homage to Devon's oak units and particularly to the early and very desirable curved cabinet, while below the purpose-built bulkhead unit also places an emphasis on natural wood. The interiors opposite are representative of slightly more contemporary offerings.

To many, the interior features of a Camper are even more important than external appearance. Personal taste plays an important part and inevitably affects potential resale values.

↑ The art of the interior is in the detail.

↘ Modern laminates give this first-generation interior a boost (left). The full nautical look. (right)

← Stunningly simple.

→ Please be seated.

FOUR CUSTOMISED EXAMPLES
FIFTH-GENERATION CAMPERS AND BEYOND

Thanks to what appears to be Volkswagen's rather relaxed approach to replacing each generation of Transporter with a new all-singing, all-dancing design, as the T5 leaves the stage, some of its clan are already a decade and more old. Those wanting something individual, a custom-built Camper, clearly had a choice. They could find a suitable donor vehicle of any age according to their budget, spend whatever monies were deemed appropriate (even splashing out on a face-lifted front* if they felt the need) and could claim to be keeping up with those ever-irritating Joneses!

Alternatively, as will soon be the case with the T6, an order could be placed at the local VW Van Centre for a brand-new model complete with all the options on your personal tick list. What became apparent during the lifespan of the T5 was the enormous increase in the number of small firms offering bespoke Camper conversions on new (or used) Transporters. For those whose DIY aspirations, or dare we say 'abilities', remain strictly limited, here was the obvious solution.

For a number of years, specialist operations will be happy to build a Camper based on the T5 to an owner's particular requirements, while it almost goes without saying that the same will be true of the T6.

* Transforming an original T5 by means of a front-end kit to the 2010-on face-lifted version would cost in the region of £1,400 at 2015 prices. The changes involve: lower bumper reinforced, upper cross member, genuine 2010-on bonnet, black and chrome radiator grille, genuine VW smooth primed bumper, genuine VW bumper inserts, twin reflector headlights.

2005 T5 WORKHORSE TO LEISURE PLEASURE VEHICLE

- Delivery Van with 2.5-litre 130PS engine finished in Ravenna Blue metallic
- Kombi-style single side windows fitted
- Bumpers and mirrors colour-coded
- Rear spoiler and window deflector
- 20in Range Rover Sport wheels and VW centre-caps
- V-Max coil-overs
- Audi TT cab seats finished in red leather, swivel arrangement for passenger seat
- Golf GTI steering wheel
- Interior panels lined with acoustic foam, floor installed and carpeted
- Crash tested rock 'n' roll rear seat/bed upholstered in cream leather with red centre panels to match the TT cab seats
- Units – wood cases, clad with high gloss veneer MDF in cream, with red edging. Chrome cupboard handles
- Smev hob/sink
- Steel roller shutter door for rear storage unit

BRAND NEW T5 TRANSPORTER (2015 MODEL) CAMPS IT UP!

Purchasers could select from seven metallic and two pearlescent shades Metallic: Natural Grey, Reflex Silver, Sand Beige, Olympia Blue, Night Blue, Toffee Brown, Blackberry Pearlescent: Deep Black Pearl, Dark Wood Pearl

The top of the range engine on offer: 2.0-litre 180PS Bi TDI, top of the range engine with VW's superb Dual Clutch Direct Shift (auto) box (seven speed)

Various trim levels including Highline, which encompasses among other items: Climatronic air conditioning, leather-covered steering wheel, gear knob and gaiter, front fogs with cornering function, alarm and immobiliser, 17in 'Thunder' alloys, rain sensor, Xenon lights, cruise control, armrests, four-way lumbar seats, body-coloured bumpers, parking sensors.

What next?
ABT Sportline fully colour-coded body kit
19in ABT alloys
30mm dropped suspension
Bespoke camper unit including twin hob, mini grill, sink and 12-volt compressor fridge
Full leather colour co-ordinated seating/ Variotech bed
Blackout blinds built into window frames
Cab captain's seats revolve
Elevating roof with built in solar panel
Built-in shower system at the rear (shower under the tailgate)
Diesel water and air heater

DECORATING A T5 (OR A T6)

On the road to customising a T5 and soon a T6, stalls at the shows or a myriad of online stores offer just about everything known to man.

Front:
- Chrome grille bumper insert
- Bull bar
- Lower front bumper spoiler
- Polished stainless-steel front grille set
- Bonnet guard hood protector

Sides
- Side steps – chromed, stainless steel or black (with LED lights)
- Side bars – chromed, polished stainless steel or black
- Tinted acrylic window wind deflector
- Stainless-steel indicator surround
- Stainless-steel fuel flap cover
- Door handles in stainless steel
- Door fingerplate in stainless steel
- Stainless-steel or chromed mirror covers

Rear
- Polished stainless-steel rear bar
- Polished stainless-steel light covers
- Tailgate spoiler
- Polished stainless-steel tailgate door handle
- Chrome-look rear bumper protector
- Polished stainless-steel tailgate edge protector
- Polished stainless-steel grab handle

Roof
- Roof rail set
- Cross bars for the above

DIFFERENT CUSTOMISING OPTIONS

Of course, the owner of a brand new van will always have plenty of options to select between. Here are three remarkably different offerings, each from suppliers offering full conversions, DIY kits, or individual components:

1. A selection of useful accessories

- Front Spoiler
- Lowering springs, axle weight to 1,550kg
- Front cab leather upholstery
- Bluetooth Touch Phone kit
- Full-length dog guard
- Pop-top roof addition

2. Full fitting service, or select and DIY

- Complete carpeting kits and 'green' friendly Insulation
- Wide range of flooring, including vinyl and wood effect from Amtico and Altro Safety flooring
- Leisure Battery and Electrics
- All upholstery, including re-upholstering front seats and rock 'roll' bed
- Template and manufacture of furniture
- Supply/fit appliances and accessories including: Smev, Dometic, Waeco, Can, Cramer, Whale, Comet, Fiamma and Thetford
- Installation of rock 'n' roll beds
- Swivel front bench seat installations
- Awnings and awning Rails
- Gas safety checks carried out by an approved engineer with written report and certification

3. For real DIY people

- MFC board or lightweight ply
- Edging catches and hinges
- Hobs and sinks, pumps and waste pipes
- Fridges and ovens
- Pre-built split charge systems
- Pumps, LED lights and switches
- Lining carpet and floor vinyl

Not to mention kits ready to install:

Bed kits
Bed with easy-fit subframe is a doddle to fit in your T5, available on track or bolted down, either design is easily removed and refitted should you want to get more than a double bed in the back of your van.

Pod kitchen
The pod kitchen kit has all you need for a simple camper or day van, comes complete with Smev sink hob combo unit , 51-litre 12V fridge, 12V control panel, 10-litre water container and pump. Choice of Formica finishes available.

Classic kit
Furniture kit consists of wardrobe and kitchen units, both with sliding doors and cut outs ready for the appliances, also a range of colour options and work surfaces to chose from. From £1,500 excluding appliances.

➜ Subtle customising of a T5 leaves a lasting impression of sophistication. Colour coding adds to the vehicle's already considerable impact.

⬇ Four T4s all sporting numerous signs of the work of cash-rich customising. No quick resprays here – even the wheels speak wealth.

A FEW WORDS ABOUT 'RAT LOOK'

Some might be tempted down the route of the 'rat look' Camper. Theoretically, any model can be given such a look, but realistically the majority seen at shows are either first- or second-generation Transporters, those rather expensive Campers most vulnerable to the ravages of the tin worm due to their age alone.

The concours purist and others might suggest that a rat look is the idle enthusiast's way of avoiding time-consuming and undoubtedly costly restorations, less onerous but still expensive panel replacement, pricey resprays and even simple washing and polishing, for the rat look involves the preservation and even the creation of additional rust.

However, while even the most dedicated rat-look fan would deny that a very small minority risk life and limb (both theirs and that of others) by cavorting around in structurally unsafe vans, the vast majority of rat-look Campers are completely sound. Indeed, many have had unparalleled monies heaped upon them in this area and that of suspension kits and meaty engines. Nor is the only too evident rust anywhere near as raw as might be expected.

The average rat-look owner may well have T-Cut his or her way

through what remains of Hanover's glossy paint until primer is exposed in the areas likely to have been polished to perfection and beyond by the dedicated owner. To accentuate the decay, the Camper will have been left out or driven in the wet, thus ensuring the formation of at least a few speckles of rust. More drastically, an owner could well have taken a sander to a panel or two and left the exposed metal to the elements. Should one or more panels be replaced, the rat-look fan will ensure that nothing more than primer is applied to it. (To aid the look, the rat-look fan will litter the glass with stickers, add battered accessories and preferably tie rope to the bumpers to give the impression that without this, the said metalwork might simply fall off.

However, a genuine rat-look fan will ensure his or her Camper's panels are afforded protection from the elements. Some resort to a monthly application of WD40 or preservative oil, but inevitably the rust appears both shiny and darker than in its natural state. Others apply a clear lacquer and this is the most effective means of preservation, providing no oil or moisture was present when the vehicle was sprayed.

Rat-look Campers are probably the most controversial of all types available on the market, falling into the 'love 'em or loathe 'em' category. Bearing this in mind, the question has to be one of value. Will a newly created rat look still carry the value it held before such action was taken?

CHAPTER 6
PIECES OF PAPER, THE
TIN WORM AND OILY BITS

If you have read and absorbed each preceding chapter of the book, you should be well on your way to making a purchase. However, the older the vehicle lined up in your mind's eye, the more significant this section will be and as a result it has been deliberately compiled to favour such buyers. While it would be possible to outline all the potential faults of a T5 engine, it is inevitable that those purchasing the extraordinarily popular generations, Campers built before the summer of 1979, will have a greater interest in such matters, or they will ensure they know someone who has. The power game, or the lack of it, before the 1970s, is straightforward, as is the condition of the interior and even the glossiness of the paint. However, for purchasers of the earlier VW Campers (and here we are extending the brief to cover the first three generations) the ever-present threat of rust can be a wallet-emptying minefield. Additionally, there is a definite need to warn of the bodged restoration. With the prices that first- and second-generation Transporters command, inevitably some people are out to make a quick buck. Buy a rusty wreck, slap filler about left, right and centre, add a glossy coat of paint and the recipe for bodging is complete.

THE RULES – THEY ARE FOR YOUR OWN GOOD

RULE 1

The first pertains to rust. If an older T5, or a T4, demonstrates evidence of rust, you walk away. In the case of the T5, it probably means it has been bashed and bodged, which you certainly don't want. There are so many immaculate examples readily available (okay, with the T4 they might be later model-year vehicles, but that shouldn't matter, as the T4 is not a historic vehicle and its long-nose guise has the best engines and, most would say, offers a more attractive stance).

Similarly, most would say that it would be sensible to walk away from a T3 with rust. The scenario is slightly different. The T3 isn't particularly valuable, so if you pay a fair price for a rusty one and have it restored, you are not going to recoup your investment. Also, there are still sufficient decent examples about (normally but not exclusively post 1985) that you don't need to purchase a rusty T3.

With the first two generations, the message is not to let your heart rule your head. Be careful how much rust you accept, unless your one aim in life is to accomplish a ground-up restoration (and you have the budget to stand it). Also, and of key importance with a first- or second-generation Transporter, don't skimp on your 'magnet and magnifying glass' search for rust in your eagerness to buy.

RULE 2

The next rule pertains to paint. If a T5 or T4 illustrates any signs of overspray, orange-peel, or mismatched panels, again you walk away and for exactly the same reasons already laid down for rust. Similarly, most would be tempted to cancel negotiations on a T3 suffering any such ailments, while for first- and second-generation models a discount should be on the cards for orange peel and mismatched panels (a defect that might be termed the responsibility of the man with the spray can rather than the owner). Overspray, on the other hand, signals careless workmanship, or an owner's lack of interest in tidying up the mess, so be prepared to abandon ship in such a case.

⬇ When considering the purchase of a VW Camper remember that they come in all sorts if conditions. Read the general rules, adapt them to suit your dreams and then stick by them. It can be expensive to break them.

RULE 3

The third rule covers both restoration and customisation. If you are considering buying a restored VW Camper, you should ask for photographic evidence of the work carried out and if that isn't available, proof of purchase of panels (and labour if the work was done by professionals). While the same makes sense for the custom fan, the additional criterion is a significant one. Is the work safe? Is the vehicle potentially dangerous? No book can tell you that because the dangers, if there are any, will be specific to the vehicle. If in doubt then engage the services of an expert (see below) and take him or her with you on a second visit, or possibly even the first.

RULE 4

The final rule has two distinct divisions but both involve not skimping on your checking or your evaluation before purchase. Everyone should go on a test drive and we would go as far as to say that this potentially jeopardises eBay (or Samba – see the next chapter) sales unless a test drive is arranged before bidding. Admittedly, if the VW Camper is a rare one, even experienced enthusiasts might be tempted to break the rules, but at least the warning has been issued.

Having eased yourself behind the wheel of your potential purchase, don't be satisfied with a brief round-the-block experience and never fall for the trick of being the passenger on a test drive. You need to

ENGAGING THE SERVICES OF AN EXPERT

If your purchase of a VW Camper will be a first for you, unless you are buying brand new or from a main VW dealer or recognised conversion company, it could well be wise to engage the services of a 'friend'.

Organisations such as the AA and RAC provide both basic and additional checks on newer vehicles, while the latter also offer a 'Prestige and Classics' service, which encompasses:

- Inspection by a brand specialist
- Full mechanical and structural inspection of the vehicle
- Underbody check
- Attention paid to known areas of concern
- Extended road test

Private individuals, marque experts or club officials might well be enticed to look at a VW Camper with you, while, if all else fails, try to convince any owner of a Transporter to tag along. Often owners are surprised what they know without realising it!

know exactly how the vehicle drives on the flat, downhill and uphill through the gears. This rule applies to all generations, regardless of age.

Remember to take more than a cursory look underneath the vehicle. Check every panel (a magnet is most useful in the detection of filler). Have a torch with you for those dark corners and never, ever be satisfied with a viewing in the wet. Rain disguises so many defects, while equally a visit in the twilight or dark is out of the question.

THE PAPER TRAIL

(This section, like the rest of the book, is written primarily with the UK purchaser in mind.)

Before purchasing, it makes sense to carry out a few checks on the vehicle; verification might cost a little money, but not taking such precautions could cost you a great deal more in both hard cash and sleepless nights.

As a starting point, you need to confirm that the VIN, chassis, engine and license plate numbers match the official registration document and that the correct owner's name is recorded on the official registration document.

Should you think of buying a T5, or conceivably but less likely a T4, from a private source there is always a danger that the vehicle has finance outstanding on it and in reality, it is not the seller's to sell. An 'HPI check' is offered by a number of companies, all of which can easily be found via the Internet.

Although it is necessary to write to the DVLA to obtain information concerning the registered keeper of a vehicle, or its previous owners, you can find out various things about the vehicle online (www. vehicleenquiry.service.gov.uk). These include:

When the current vehicle tax expires, the date the vehicle was first registered, its SORN status, the colour, its engine size, year of manufacture, fuel type, CO_2 emissions and the current vehicle tax rate.

Other internet sources offer a wider field of information. Here's a snippet from one such homepage:

If you are purchasing a used vehicle, do you really know what you are buying? Is the vehicle stolen? Perhaps it has been written off? Is the mileage correct? Is there outstanding finance? We can answer these questions and many more, putting your mind at rest and potentially saving you thousands with our comprehensive car registration checks. Our car check information comes from a number of sources including the Police National Computer for recorded stolen vehicles (PNC), the DVLA and the Association of British Insurers (ABI).

EVALUATION
TOPIC BY TOPIC

Assuming you are buying a nearly new VW Camper from an official
VW dealer, or from a widely recognised conversion company, your
evaluation process is going to be much truncated in comparison to
that of someone considering a first-, second-, or even third-generation
Camper. As it has already been advised that you should walk away from
a newer VW Camper exhibiting any sign of rust, defective paint etc., this
evaluation inevitably concentrates on the older generations.

PAINTING AND DECORATING

Looking at a VW Camper's paint is always a good place to start,
and while you're about it whatever trim it carries. Poor paintwork is
usually a sign of neglect, neglect that can have hidden and serious
consequences. In the same manner, rusty trim, dull brightwork, faded
plastics are all things that can be avoided in the first instance and easily
replaceable in the second.

■ INSPECTING THE PAINT

Realistically very few first- or second-generation Transporters will carry
their original coats of Volkswagen's high-quality paint. Of those that
do it is likely that some of the more vulnerable panels will have been
resprayed once or more during the vehicle's lengthy lifetime.

If your motive for purchase is concours competition, apart from
the vehicle being presented in its original shade, whether repainted or
not, the key issue will be one of original and resprayed panels being a
perfect match, or where a total respray has taken place that the colour
is accurate to the original.

Assuming the aim of buying a VW Camper is to camp in it, the colour
is no longer of the utmost significance. Indeed, quite a number of VW
Campers used for camping are finished in highly attractive but non-
original shades. Likewise, the interest in a customised Camper is not
the originality of the shade but in the perfection of the application and
quite often, the radical nature of the colour chosen.

Common paint 'faults' include the following, most of which can
be remedied – at a price. The more serious the issue, the greater the
discount on the asking price you need to demand (unless the purchase
price already reflects such a problem).

1) The 'orange peel' effect is caused by the failure of atomised
paint droplets to flow into each other when they make contact with the

metal. The use of paint cutting or rubbing compound, or even very fine grades of abrasive paper, might well resolve the problem. A great deal depends on how fussy you are, particularly when it has been known for manufacturers (obviously not members of the Volkswagen family) to offer cars afflicted by this ailment direct from the factory.

2) Cracking can be attributed to a variety of causes, one of the most common being either too heavy an application of filler before the paint, or of the gloss coat/s. Failure to mix the paint thoroughly before application can cause the same result, as can a reaction between what was already on the VW Camper and the new paint. On occasion, the paint finish appears crazed rather than showing obvious signs of cracking. The causes remain the same and in all cases, the only option is to remove all the affected paint and respray once more.

3) Micro-blistering occurs usually as a result of moisture settling on the vehicle after rubbing down, or sanding back to bare metal and before paint application. Home resprays, or economy jobs, where insufficient heating has been available, are the usual sources of this affliction, although covering/protecting a vehicle with material that doesn't 'breathe' can lead to the same result. The only solution is to respray the affected areas.

4) Dimples in the paint are usually the result of a residue of polish not being removed properly before painting. Again, the only solution

↑ Overspray simply isn't acceptable, a sign of an economy job, a rushed project, a quick fix ... walk away please. (Come to think of it, moss doesn't bode well either!)

⬆ Bubbling and cracking – the most serious of paint troubles – is a sign that the tin worm has burrowed and is about to hatch. The yellow van is full of filler, while there is obvious filler and seam rust on the blue-grey one.

is to remove the paint, prepare the vehicle thoroughly and repaint it. Peeling, on the other hand, tends either to be the result of poor application or, in the case of some metallic finishes, where the sealing lacquer has been damaged. Again, the only solution is to start again.

Three further paint issues are slightly different, one very serious and two possibly remedied without substantial cost.

1) Fading, an occurrence particularly associated with the colour red, is the result of exposure to the sun (and an attendant lack of polish protection). Providing the damage isn't too pronounced, paint restorers, or even the careful use of rubbing or cutting compounds, can restore the vehicle to its original glory.

2) Small dents of a recent nature can often be 'pulled out' by tradesmen offering such services. For once, they are more likely to come to you, rather than you having to go to them. Of course, such an operator can't work miracles, and if the paint surface has been damaged and either primer or bare metal exposed, a different course of action will have to be taken.

3) The serious one is called blistering or bubbling and the

consequences of overlooking it, or opting to ignore it, will be costly. The damage to the gloss surface is caused by rust beneath the paint and on even a cursory probe (assuming the owner will let you) will undoubtedly reveal more serious rust problems than the number of blisters imply. Filler and further paint is not the answer. The panels afflicted will have either to be repaired or replaced.

■ ALL THE TRIMMINGS

Realistically the average VW Camper, whether it is a first-, second- or third-generation, won't be over-endowed with shiny brightwork. All first- and virtually every second-generation Transporter featured painted bumpers and only top-of-the-range early T3 models were favoured with a smudging of chrome (black painted metal, or later moulded plastic, being the norm). Likewise, as many pre-1979 Camper conversions were based on the Kombi and later on the even lowlier Delivery Van, painted hubcaps were the order of the day. Only examples offered on the Micro Bus or its De Luxe counterpart could claim an original provenance for chrome. During the lifetime of the T3, shiny hubcaps became unfashionable and were replaced by either plastic centre caps or plastic wheel discs. Anodised brightwork too suffered a marked decline.

In summary, if what bright bits there are appear tarnished/rusty or simply aged, the cost of replacement isn't going to break the bank (NOS originals won't be cheap, though, just as reproductions from reputable sources will hurt the credit card). The point, however, is that a vehicle presented for sale shouldn't have shoddy trim whether it is faded, untreated plastic, scraped and rusty bumpers, tarnished or potted chrome, or anodised brightwork. Such items are a warning sign that other more serious areas of neglect might be lurking to bite you later.

IN SEARCH OF THE TIN WORM – THE GUIDED TOUR

The search for rust is one of the most important areas of your evaluation and particularly so the older the vehicle is. Please remember that protection against rust was not a consideration of motor manufacturers in the 1950s, 1960s and 1970s and was in its infancy during the following decade. Indeed, if a T3 is your chosen VW Camper, it has already been said more than once that you would be wisest to purchase a later model, as from the middle of the decade protection against rust was finally added to Volkswagen's agenda.

The best way to hunt the tin worm is to be logical, even though rust in some areas is more dangerous to the well-being of the VW Camper (and your wallet) than others. The suggestion is that you work from the top downwards, leaving the delights of crawling under the Camper until last.

Starting at the top then, plain and simple roof panels are invariably sound, although the same cannot be said of those fitted with an elevating roof. Where these have leaked, if not like a sieve then certainly with intermittent drips, the damage won't be to the roof panel but to the associated structure inside the Camper. An elevating roof of any sort ought to be checked thoroughly, as repairs to, or replacement of, this useful addition to the Camper's specification are costly exercises.

⬇ Roof and guttering issues – whether it's a hole in the roof panel (or a big blister) or crumbling gutters, there is no quick makeover that will be satisfactory for more than a few months. Beware!

Roof gutters, a standard feature of older VW Campers, are prone to rust, either of the creeping variety, or the straightforward crumbling type. The metalwork of the gutter folds back onto the main section of the roof panel, but with age, or possibly a lack of attention, creeping surface rust emerges from the seam. The likelihood of finding a vehicle with crumbling gutters and no other rust on its body is remote. The damage can be repaired – the question has to be, how many moths are you prepared to release from the wallet?

The panels surrounding the side and rear windows tend to be in good order, although dubious examples of earlier third-generation Transporters can be the exception to this rule. The metalwork below the windscreen is another matter altogether but one more-or-less confined to second-generation Transporters. The design of the lower edge of the window surround allows water to collect under the window rubber; rust occurs with amazing regularity and particularly so on vehicles where the rubber has perished or split.

The front panels on earlier models are inevitably prone to stone-chips owing to their slab-like nature and the sheer extent of metalwork exposed to the road (due to a lack of a radiator grille and the absence of a traditional bonnet). Untreated damage inevitably leads to greater areas of rust (but there are those who varnish the rust and revel in the aged look of the vehicle). Unfortunately, in the case of the T3, there is an additional tin-worm issue adjoining the front panel. Predictably, the

⬇ A weathered front panel can be rectified. One that has suffered a shunt with another vehicle isn't going to be as easy.

↑ The metalwork below the windscreen isn't bad on this second-generation Transporter, but at least you know where to look. Stone-chips on the front panel turn to blisters if left untreated ...

↗ T3 rust trap behind the front bumper. Bodge it and it will be back.

flat metalwork situated behind the front bumper forms a water trap, which in turn attracts the tin worm.

Similarly, the inset design of the metalwork surrounding the headlamp on all second-generation Transporters tends to result in rust formation, aided by the tin worm's desire to creep from behind the chrome trim ring.

Moving to the sides of the vehicle, three notable defects immediately spring to mind. The first concerns doors, both of the cab and side-loading variety. The second, which has two linked parts to its name, may look innocuous but masks much more serious trouble. The third is peculiar to the T3 and a failing that you must already be familiar with by now.

As you might expect, doors tend to suffer from blocked drainage holes, which allows moisture to build up and the tin worm to hatch. Both replacement doors and rust-free examples from sunny climes are readily available for most years, but as many restorers need them, the prices are predictably firm. (As a worthwhile aside, check the side door channel. A sliding side door was a standard feature on second- and third-generation Transporters and an option for later first-generation models. If the channel has rusted and crumbled, the door could simply fall off in your hands.)

Usually, the doors of a third-generation Transporter will be in better condition than those of its predecessors; if only the same could be said of the seams. Here's the story once more. In what proved to be a futile attempt to preserve the T3's paintwork and panels, Volkswagen filled the seams with a sealer in the assembly process. Unfortunately,

➜ Fairly obvious really – this door has rust and someone has tried to disguise it with filler – no chance!

➜ Fortunately, doors from drier countries are readily available depending on the age of the Transporter. Of course, many people want them, so they don't go cheap.

⬆ T3 seam rust aggravated in the top right picture by proximity to the fuel filler and inevitable dribbles – please walk away immediately! Middle left – 'rat-look' with the wheel arches clearly visible in the battered side panel and middle right – an 'old girl' from the fifties portraying the same ailment. Trouble ahead thanks to the rot and rust behind.

⬅ Caught on camera during the restoration process, this Camper has undergone extensive surgery, work that won't have come cheap but will be worth it in the future. Of course, it might be better to purchase a Camper that doesn't require work in the first place…

this sealer becomes brittle with age and tends to fall out, creating an ideal breeding ground for the tin worm. Likewise, if fuel has been spilt, as often happens, when plying the T3 with petrol or diesel, protective polish is dissolved, and some of the worst seam rust is evident in the vicinity of the fuel cap. This kind of rust is difficult to get rid of, and a third-generation Transporter so afflicted should be avoided at all cost.

Returning to the first- and second-generation Transporters, a visible outline of the rear wheel arch in the form of rust implies non-too-carefully masked trouble, as does a hole or evidence of the tin worm in the lower right, rear quarter panel.

This latter imperfection relates to a rotting battery tray (situated to the right of the engine bay), initially caused by leaking corrosive battery acid. As for the outline of the rear wheel arch, this is a result of corrosion in its seam and invariably indicative of further problems underneath the vehicle, each of which will be outlined shortly.

Turning to the vehicle's rear, the engine compartment hinges on post-March 1955 first-generation Transporters and all second-generation models, stand proud and are therefore prone to rust. Campers from the 1972 model year and later have a fixed rear valance (as opposed to the earlier version, which unbolts) and the seams joining it to the rear quarter panels tend to rust.

⬇ Rear quarter panel rust – that evident in the right hand one might have been caused by corrosive acid leaking from the battery/tray.

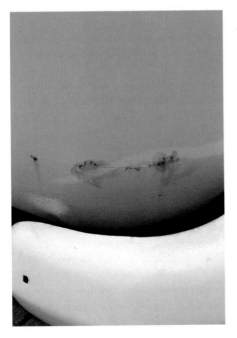

↑ Always lift the mats in the cab – plenty of metal to rot here.

Any concours judge worthy of his title, or any purchaser of a VW Camper, will want to spend time assessing the condition of the underneath of the vehicle. Initial clues can be found by looking at the cab step and by lifting the mats in the cab surrounding the driver and passenger seats. Likewise, examine the area where the cab floor joins the vehicle's front panel, as this is another part of the Camper vulnerable to the ravages of the tin worm.

Before crawling underneath the vehicle (something that shouldn't be avoided), check for deterioration in the condition of the somewhat vulnerable panels behind the front wheels. If either or both of these are rotten, there is more trouble ahead.

While kneeling or bent double, have a good look at the sills. Although not a contributory factor to a failed MOT, if the tin worm has a hold, here's confirmation of your diagnosis concerning those front wheel panels and a reason to crawl under the vehicle post haste. Once under the Camper, look at the underbody protection plates (where fitted), the condition of the longitudinal chassis rails and the attendant outriggers (and particularly so the ends), the suspension mounting points and the torsion-bar tubes (particularly where the outer uprights join the tube). Replacement of any of the above, if they are suspect, will not only be essential but also expensive. Please note that you cannot and must not attempt to weld the torsion bar tubes and that rusty torsion bar tubes are an MOT failure point.

↑ A first-generation Transporter without its clothes.

← Always check the wheel-arch panel behind the front wheel.

↙ The longitudinal chassis members must always be examined.

↓ A partly restored first-generation Transporter photographed from the rear of the vehicle looking towards the still-unrestored bulkhead panel. Longitudinal chassis members and supporting outriggers are clearly visible.

A final point to note is one concerning a bus that has been welded. You need to make sure that the work has been done to an appropriate standard, while also checking that dollops of filler haven't been plastered on to disguise rust temporarily. If you were suspicious about any of the vehicle's panels, no doubt the magnet was in use. There is absolutely no reason why the magnet shouldn't be used on the underneath of the vehicle. It would be wise to be suspicious of a new and remarkably thick layer of underbody protection, just in case it has been daubed on to mask a multitude of sins. Of course, should there be evidence of an annual coating of Waxoyl, or other proprietary protective measures, the percentage risk of tin-worm attacks will be significantly reduced.

⬇ Rusty reminders – taunting the tin worm. Before and after – more expense (below left and right). Time to order a replacement door (bottom).

🏹 Repaired rear quarter panel
– think battery tray.

⬆ Is this as bad as it looks? Think longitudinal chassis members and outriggers and perhaps the 'living area' floor isn't as significant.

⬅ Rust on a T4 – find another one!

⬇ If you ever come across a Camper filled with filler like this one, run away as fast as you can. It will bite!

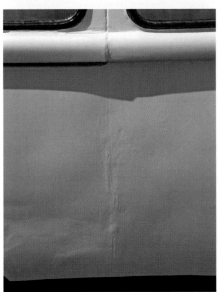

SHINY TRIM, THE SPARKLE OF
GLASS AND LET THERE BE LIGHT

Although none of the categories covered here are anyway near as significant as the VW Camper's body panels and their potential to cost a fortune in the eradication of rust, when assessing a vehicle for purchase, there's no point in being blasé about such topics.

The concours entrant will want to ensure that all the trim is correct for the year and when it is of a shiny nature that it is polished to perfection. Hubcaps, script badges and even the famous VW roundel are all readily available, while if a vehicle has good paintwork and panels, its trim is also likely to be in good condition.

Extending the trim category to window rubbers, wipers and the like, opens the field to more serious issues. If the window rubbers are perished or cracked, they should be replaced. The quality of some reproduction sets of window rubbers has been questioned, premature aging or perishing being the main issues, while fitting any window rubber (and in certain instances associated brightwork) is not the easiest of tasks. Meanwhile wiper blades should wipe and there is no excuse for them not doing so. Wiper arms are available although inevitably the older the vehicle, the more costly the replacement is likely to be.

Scratched window glass is irritating, while a chipped screen is a potential MOT failure. Glass for most ages of VW Camper is available and particularly so on the second-hand market. On occasion, a fully restored vehicle can be let down by the shabby nature of the glass (there speaks the concours judge).

The first-generation Transporter featured 6-volt electrics until its final year of German production. Renowned for producing lights with a candlelight glow, many owners have had their vehicle upgraded to 12-volt. Such a consideration apart, tarnished or rusted reflectors will result in an MOT reprimand. The various light housings, both front and rear, are more readily available the newer the vehicle is. Such items for early first-generation models can be picked up at vintage shows (most notably those held in Germany), but the process can be eye-wateringly expensive at such events.

If a vehicle is fitted with semaphore indicators (pre-1961 model-year vehicles for the European market and those manufactured before April 1955 for VW Campers destined for the USA), they must be in good working order, although serious consideration ought to be given to adding bumper-mounted modern (but of period appearance) flashers. Most drivers on the road won't recall the era of the semaphore, while sadly a percentage simply couldn't care less (in their haste to get from A to B in record time) that yours is a historic vehicle.

WHEELS AND TYRES (INCLUDING THE OILY BITS THEY DEPEND ON)

The majority of this section relates to the earlier generations of Transporter and is really only of relevance to the would-be owner of a VW Camper who wishes to enter a concours, or keep his or her vehicle in the form it left Wolfsburg, or more likely Hanover, many years ago.

All Transporters were fitted with cross-ply tyres until August 1971 although even then some 1600 engine models were not endowed with radials. (As usual, there is an exception to the rule. Second-generation Micro Bus De Luxe models were shod with radials from their inception in August 1967.)

Both first- and second-generation Transporters were fitted with steel wheels of a five-bolt design. Initially 16 inches in diameter and minus any form of ventilation slot, from March 1955 they were reduced to 15 inches and carried four wide ventilation slots between the rim and the centre of the wheel. From August 1963, these slots became narrower, as the diameter of the wheel was reduced by a further inch to 14. (Tyres, first generation: to March 1955, 5.50x16; to July 1963, 6.40x15; to end of production, 7.00x14.) Second-generation Transporters were shod with 5Jx14 wheels until August 1970 and with 5½x14 thereafter. Twenty circular ventilation holes replaced the previous ventilation slots and were introduced in August 1970 to coincide with the introduction of front disc brakes, and 185x14 radial tyres were standard.

Third-generation Transporters were the first to be fitted with alloy wheels as standard, but the allocation was strictly limited to luxury models. Two general points arise from this, both of which are applicable to all generations. Wherever a set of alloy wheels has been fitted, either as part of the original specification, as an option or accessory marketed by Volkswagen, or simply by a previous owner, check that they haven't been 'kerbed' as this will be reasonably expensive to rectify. Similarly, check steel wheels for evidence of buckling, as not only is this potentially dangerous but also, as this is caused by hitting a kerb, suspension components may have been damaged too.

Badly pitted steel wheels can be a nightmare to rid of rust and this concours judge at least won't be sympathetic. Even if concours isn't an ambition, unsightly wheels let the side down – replica Porsche 356 ones might be a palatable compromise as they neither look too modern for the vehicle, nor so dull in appearance that you may well think your money has been wasted.

DECIDEDLY
OILY MATTERS

Many purchasers might either leave the next segment of the evaluation to an independent assessor, a knowledgeable friend they have cajoled into joining them, or simply risk noticing something amiss at the test-drive stage. It might also be assumed that the more mechanically adept will purchase a first- or second-generation Transporter, and for that reason alone the emphasis is placed on such models in what follows.

Arrange with the seller to have the front of the vehicle lifted safely onto axle stands. Grab the wheel at the top and bottom and rock it. If any play is detected then grab the wheel at each side and rock it again. If there is no play now then there is wear on the king and/or link pins in the case of a first-generation model, or in the stub axle swivel joints of a second-generation model. If there is play in both directions then the wheel bearings will need attention. Spin the wheel and if the bearings are noisy then they are worn or damaged and will need replacing; if there is no noise then it should be possible to take up the play with adjustment.

Finally, having positioned the steering in the straight-ahead position, turn the steering wheel first to the left and then to the right. Movement of more than 2.5 to 3.0cm before the wheels react is indicative if a steering box that requires adjustment at best, or, more expensively, replacement.

ENGINES, GEARBOXES AND THE BITS
THAT HELP THE VW CAMPER GO

The big thing to remember here is that, unless your passion is tinkering with oily bits, you can always purchase a new engine, or the components necessary to make the existing one feel like new. If you can afford to buy a decent first-generation Camper, or a pristine second-generation model, a replacement engine is not going to break the bank.

■ THE ENGINE

The first telltale sign that something is amiss is if the engine is covered in oil (a factor which applies to all generations) and the lid and compartment of air-cooled Campers is smeared with a black film. The engine must be switched off before you carry out what is an essential check on air-cooled engines. Grasp the crankshaft pulley and push/pull it forwards and backwards. If more than the slightest movement is detected, your worst suspicions are likely to be confirmed and the engine will need a rebuild.

Similarly, if the fan/generator belt is slack, there is a distinct possibility that it will have been slipping, which will have resulted in a lack of adequate cooling. This is serious in an air-cooled engine, with consequences ranging from a cracked cylinder head to cracked or broken pistons and rings.

Another essential check concerns the rubber seals around the engine tinware and all the tubing. If these are either missing or in a dilapidated state, it is likely that heat from the exhaust system will have been drawn into the engine fan, meaning that the cylinders and heads may not have been cooled properly and the engine will have overheated on several occasions as a result. Second-generation Transporters have a foam surround between the engine and its tinware. Check that this isn't damaged, as it is possible that any loose bits have been drawn into the fan, which can lead to blockage and overheating.

■ CARBURETTORS/FUEL INJECTION

Generally, the older the Transporter and its carburettor, the more simple it will be in design. Attempts to reduce pollution resulted in more complex and potentially troublesome later carbs (also note that the larger 1700, 1800 and 2.0-litre engines were endowed with twin carburettors in Europe – see below). However, age can result in the throttle spindle becoming sloppy, which causes air leaks and the loss of a little fuel. An inevitable result will be poor running. Check wear by rocking the spindle backwards and forwards.

A large number of carburettors have been replaced over the years. Ideally, a rebuilt Solex carburettor should be the choice (and definitely so if your aim is to impress a concours judge), but a good number of Transporters have been fitted with Weber carbs.

From an insistence in the early 1970s by the State of California that Volkswagens should be fitted with less-polluting fuel-injection systems, the whole of the USA took this on board. As a result, you could well find either an 1800 or 2.0-litre US-market second-generation Transporter so endowed (once the larger engines were introduced, unlike Europe, the smaller 1600 engine was deleted from the option list).

Although both twin carburettors and the non-direct fuel-injection system didn't have a reputation for particular problems, their respective complexities demand that all but the most skilled amateurs (who also possesses the necessary tools) seek professional help if anything goes wrong.

■ ENGINE LEAKS

This topic has already been touched upon, but here a little further advice is given to those considering the purchase of a first- or second-generation Transporter. The key point is whether the engine and its surroundings are covered in oil.

Dribbles of oil at the top of the engine might be due to something as simple as the owner not taking sufficient care when topping up, but also you should consider the following:

- Black tin surrounding the oil filler tube rusted through or loose
- Perished oil cooler seals
- Worn pistons and piston rings

If there is oil apparent underneath the engine where it joins the transmission, it is likely that the crankshaft oil seal is to blame. The other possibility is that the gearbox shaft seal requires replacement.

Oil to the right of the engine will be either from the valve cover gasket, or the result of a leaking push rod tube oil seal. While in this vicinity, check to see if the thermostat and its attendant cooling control flaps have been removed. Some owners think this to be a good idea, being of the erroneous opinion that cooling will be improved. However, the thermostat is there to ensure that the engine warms up quickly to its most efficient temperature, and the flaps are there to direct the cooling air over and between the cylinders.

When checking the left-hand side of the engine for the same leaks, also look above the pushrod tubes for evidence of oil. If this is the case, the chief suspect will be the oil cooler/push rod seals once more. However, it is possible that the crankcase is cracked, which is serious and will require an engine rebuild.

■ THE EXHAUST/HEAT EXCHANGERS

The exhaust attached to an air-cooled engine is not a long-lived item, with some suggesting no more than a two-year lifespan. Dependent on the year, some original equipment items are now few and far between, while sadly some copies are not particularly well made. From 1963, all Transporters were fitted with heat exchangers, the purpose of which is to transfer air generated by the engine into the interior of the Transporter. This is achieved by passing a proportion of the air from the cooling fan through flexible ducts, through the tinware at the rear of the engine and then into the heat-exchanger 'pods', which surround the exhaust pipes (note that the air being heated should not come into contact with the exhaust gases!). Now heated by the hot exhaust pipes, the warm air travels through a long tube to the front of the vehicle for distribution via dashboard controls.

Genuine exchangers are difficult to come by these days and expensive if they can be found. However, some replacement parts are made using cost-cutting methods, but the result is invariably a Camper cab that is never really warm. Visibly corroded heat exchangers will need replacing.

■ THE GEARBOX

Volkswagen Camper gearboxes are robust no matter which generation you might be considering. If during your test drive, the vehicle slips out of gear (including reverse) a new gearbox will most likely be required. However, specialist firms exist who can rebuild earlier gearboxes.

Most problems associated with the first-generation Transporter are driveshaft related, with the swing axles being troubled by leaky driveshaft gaiters, or worn-out or leaking reduction boxes (reduction boxes, only a feature of the first-generation Transporter, are designed to reduce the gearing and increase the ride height). Double-jointed driveshafts, as fitted to the second- and third-generation Transporter models, are prone to worn constant velocity joints, or split joint gaiters.

A sign that all is not well with an automatic gearbox (introduced in 1972 for the '73 model year) is poor acceleration and a failure to reach maximum speed. The likely causes are either incorrect torque converter fluid level, or a faulty torque converter. Automatic gearbox repairs tend to be specialist territory, while it should be noted that for many years the performance of a VW Camper without a clutch was always pedestrian in comparison to that of one with a manual gearbox. (Budding T4 owners should note that the automatic VR6/V6 was more than adequate in performance terms as might be expected, while T5 hopefuls might be wise to consider Volkswagen's dual clutch 'automatic' option. DSG finally quashed the wails of the anti-automatic lobby, Volkswagen often suggesting 0–60mph performance to be faster than with a manual gearbox.

■ THE BATTERY

There is little to say here, other than to note that a battery with corrosion on the terminals is probably past its sell-by date, while beware the unscrupulous seller who has charged the battery just before you are due to visit.

■ TRANSPORTER ELECTRICS

Please remember that European market first-generation Transporters carried 6-volt electrics until the final year of production, the '67 model year, although 12-volt electrics had been available earlier as an extra-cost option. Many owners decide to upgrade to the notably more acceptable 12-volt system for today's driving conditions. If a conversion has taken place, make sure the work has been carried out to a professional standard. Avoid vehicles showing evidence of a multitude of crimped insulated spade connectors, a web of non-standard wires in a variety of colours and worst of all, tap connectors (also known as 'Scotch-lock' connectors), which have always been intended for temporary repairs only.

TECH SPEC OF A FIRST-GENERATION TRANSPORTER

First-generation Transporter – 1500 engine, generally available from March 1963, slightly revised from August 1965 (as shown here)

- ■ Four-cylinder, four stroke, horizontally opposed, in the rear of the vehicle.
- ■ Bore and Stroke: 83mm x 69mm
- ■ Capacity: 1,493cc
- ■ Compression ratio: 7.5:1
- ■ Maximum output: 44PS @ 4,000rpm

- ■ Top speed and cruising speed: 65mph (limited by a governor from August 1964)
- ■ From a 1964 US market brochure: The Volkswagen's new air-cooled engine has a 25 per cent larger displacement, produces 25 per cent more horsepower than the engine it replaces. It can push a fully loaded VW wagon up 28 per cent grades. Or drive along the highway at a speed of 65mph. A single-throat downdraft carburettor with an accelerator pump gives you a quick pickup when you need it, yet keeps fuel consumption low. And the new engine still averages about 24 miles to a gallon of regular gas.

← Here is Volkswagen's delightful over-technical image of the 1500 engine as presented in a good number of mid-1960s brochures. Not only is the flat-four engine dissected but also the gearbox, while even the heating arrangements are on view.

■ ENGINE SPECIFICATION GUIDE ACROSS THE GENERATIONS

Sorry, as a potential T5 owner, you might be feeling a little left out and sadly this is likely to persist if only because the specification of the best 'early' fifth-generation engine has already been outlined elsewhere. However, working on the principle that things always change for the better, the spec for the later and most-powerful T5 common-rail engine is included in the line-up of what some might suggest is the best 'original' engine for each generation of VW Camper.

It is also worth adding that a number of firms carry the parts necessary to rebuild the earlier engines, while others will do the job for you. Likewise, there are companies dedicated to building and supplying bigger engines than Volkswagen ever intended.

TECH SPEC OF A SECOND-GENERATION TRANSPORTER

Second-generation Transporter 2.0-litre engine, available from August 1975

■ Four-cylinder, four stroke, horizontally opposed, in the rear of the vehicle.
■ Bore and Stroke: 94.0mm x 71.0mm
■ Capacity: 1,970cc
■ Compression ratio: 7.3:1
■ Maximum output: 70PS @ 4,200rpm
■ Top speed and cruising speed: 80mph

■ From a 1978 South African market brochure: We call our Microbus 2000L the Musclebus. And with good reason. A husky 1970cm³ engine makes this the most powerful VW Microbus range ever. There's power to spare 51.0kw – for effortless all-day speed-limit cruising. For whisking up the steepest of hills. And there is loads of torque for big loads ...
■ Average fuel consumption: 22.6mpg

← Volkswagen's 'suitcase' engine, originally designed for the VW 1500 saloon (a sort of larger Beetle). Volkswagen used the same image in Transporter brochures whether they were offering a 1700cc, 1800cc or 2.0-litre unit.

TECH SPEC OF A THIRD-GENERATION TRANSPORTER

Third-generation Transporter – 2.1-litre petrol engine, available from 1985.

■ Four-cylinder, horizontally opposed OHV water-cooled, in the rear of the vehicle (Petrol, Digi-jet fuel injection).
■ Bore and Stroke: 94.0mm x 71.0mm
■ Capacity: 2,109cc
■ Compression ratio: 10.5:1
■ Maximum output: 112 PS @ 4,800rpm
■ Maximum speed: 94mph

■ From a 1990 Canadian market brochure (note this market featured a version of the 2.1-litre petrol engine with catalytic converter, which reduced maximum output): A rear-mounted, rear-wheel drive, 2.1 litre Digifant fuel injection engine, matched with power rack and pinion steering and fully independent front and rear suspension help produce superb handling and an exceptional, sedan-like ride ...
■ Average fuel consumption 21.9 mpg

⬇ The T3's unique range of water-cooled petrol engines, together with the diesels on offer in the mid to late 1980s.

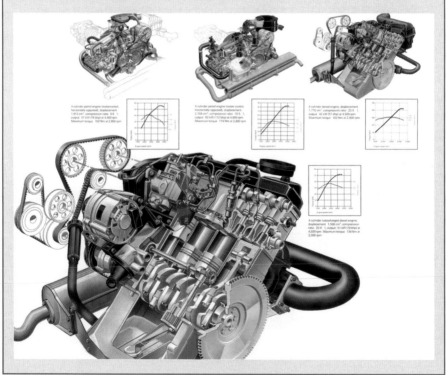

210

TECH SPEC OF A FOURTH-GENERATION TRANSPORTER

Fourth-generation Transporter – 2.5-litre TDI diesel engine, available from 1996

- Five-cylinder in-line turbocharged direct-injection (hence TDI) diesel mounted at the front of the vehicle.
- Bore and Stroke: 81.0mm x 95.5mm
- Capacity: 2,459cc
- Compression ratio: 19.5:1
- Maximum output: 102PS @ 3,500 rpm
- Top speed and cruising speed: 98mph
- From a 1997 British-market brochure: The new 2.5TDI engine makes the Caravelle more powerful and more economical at the same time. Drivers will love the 250Nm of torque that is available at engine speeds between 1,900 and 2,300rpm. This 2.5-litre,

5-cylinder, direct-injection, turbocharged and intercooled engine delivers 102bhp. Driving characteristics give a distinctly high-performance feel ... Its remarkable smoothness makes an important contribution to passenger comfort, and extensive sound insulation work in the engine compartment, together with improved engine mounts, has ensured that the noise level is very well subdued. Owners will also be impressed by the economy of the TDI. At a constant 56mph a fuel consumption of 42.8mpg has been recorded. An average fuel consumption of 35.8mpg is also possible, depending on load and traffic conditions.

↑ The 2.5TDI diesel engine, powerful and economical all in one.

← Volkswagen's Press Office still keeps imagery of the V6 engines on file.

TECH SPEC OF A FIFTH-GENERATION TRANSPORTER

Fifth-generation Transporter – 2.0-litre BiTDI – new range of engines available from January 2010 in the UK

- Four-cylinder in-line twin-turbo direct-injection diesel mounted at the front of the vehicle.
- Bore and Stroke: 81.0mm x 95.5mm
- Capacity: 1,968cc
- Compression ratio: 16.5:1
- Maximum output: 180PS @ 4,000 rpm
- Maximum torque: 295lb ft @ 1,500–2,000rpm
- Top speed and cruising speed: 119mph
- 0–60mph: 11.4 seconds
- From the 2015 model year brochure for the British market: Our renowned TDI engines have long been setting the standards in diesel technology – and with rising fuel costs, we've

also been working hard to lower fuel consumption, while reducing CO_2 emissions. The California range reflects this with a choice of three 2.0-litre common-rail diesel engines, all complying with Euro 5 emission limits and equipped with diesel particulate filters as standard.

- 2.0-LITRE 132kW (180PS) BiTDI ENGINE As the most powerful engine in the range, the amazing 180PS BiTDI diesel engine features BiTurbo (BiTDI) technology and produces an incredible 400Nm maximum torque. This results in a driving experience that's second to none. This engine is available with a 6-speed manual gearbox or 7-speed dual clutch direct shift gearbox (DSG), while 4MOTION can also be specified.
- Average fuel consumption: 35.8mpg

← Powerful and efficient engines for the facelift T5 of 2010 and onwards.

ALL THE THINGS TO CHECK ABOUT AN INTERIOR NOT MENTIONED ELSEWHERE

The interior is the distinguishing feature of a Camper conversion carried out by a recognised company, just as any customised vehicle must have an inspirational inside to be noticed. What will be assessed here are those features common to all Transporters – Camper, Delivery Van or People Carrier. With five generations and 65 years of production to assess, an alphabetic list hopefully proves helpful, although the detail of the observations tend to be orientated towards the older VW Campers.

■ DASHBOARD AND INSTRUMENT PANEL

Dashboards started life as no more than a single instrument binnacle (all models except the Micro Bus De Luxe) but in 1955 were extended to a full-length all-metal affair. Metal continued to predominate into the era of the second-generation Transporter, but with the new model of the summer of 1979 there also came plastic in profusion. Points to note are that the older the plastic, the more it is likely to crack/split due to brittleness caused by exposure to sunlight. The gadgetry of more modern dashes is susceptible to clumsy hands and sausage fingers, so beware. Hacking a hole in a dash of any age to accommodate modern ICE (in-car-entertainment) systems is sacrilege, but it does happen and can be costly to remedy. Old – 1950s and '60s – genuine accessories can be worth a fortune, but please remember that someone hasn't removed the fuel gauge if the VW Camper was manufactured before 1961 – there wasn't one!

■ DOOR CARDS AND TRIM PANELS

The main point to make here is one of warping and obvious signs of water issues. While damaged door cards (they tend to suffer more than trim panels) can be replaced and original-style cards with trim are available, the issue has to be one of why the panel is warped in the first place. Tears and splits tend to indicate an unloved Camper, which in turn might spell other trouble. Dirt removal on vinyl is easy (just be careful that whatever proprietary brand of cleaner you use doesn't leave a white hue everywhere); cloth tends to be trickier.

■ HANDLES, WINDERS AND MORE MODERN DEVICES

While door handles (originally painted, or chromed, metal and later plastic-coated metal and later still, simply plastic) and window winders tend to be fairly robust, but the same can't be said of the latter's winder mechanism (hidden in the door) when they are made of plastic. Wind up and wind down to check is about all you can do (but note that a first-generation Transporter will have sliding, nail-breaking, cab-door windows). Much more modern electric windows can fail too, and all you can do is check that they work. Early quarter-light catches can be suspect and wouldn't stop any self-respecting thief, while the chunkier ones afforded second-generation Transporters need checking. Damaged or completely wrecked ones are more than a nuisance and fiddly to replace.

■ FLOOR COVERINGS

The older the VW Camper, the more the likelihood of the cab floor having originally been carpeted in rubber. Whatever type the floor covering is, lift it where you can to assess the state of what is underneath. You should be wary of stains (and downright suspicious of damp coverings) that imply leaks and it is always preferable to see that an owner has covered the floor with footwell mats. If you can lift the floor coverings of the 'living' area of a Camper, do so, as the same rules apply. However, many floors will have been officially, or unofficially, lined and tiled, or covered in a laminate. Do your best!

■ HEADLINING

From hardboard (or cloth for the more de luxe offerings), Volkswagen progressed to vinyl and later still to today's fabric-coated panels. Later headlinings, vinyl onwards, are subject to either rips or marks and gouges, while cloth from the 1950s and early 1960s could well have rotted. A new wool headlining is not easy to fit, but there are those who will do it for you. Retaining, for example, the birch-wood lining of a 1960s Westfalia Camper, richer in colour than when it was new, adds to the appeal of the vehicle, but a stained or torn vinyl headlining is usually a candidate for replacement. Dirt on a vinyl headlining is easy to deal with and as most are white, virtually any cleaner can be used. However, if a stain has a yellowy hue, the likelihood is that the Transporter was owned by a smoker and sadly, the ravages of nicotine abuse will not be removable. Don't even think about painting the headlining – it doesn't work! Replacement linings are available but are far from easy to fit. Marks on later fabric-coated panels can be removed with soap and water (but not too much of either) and be careful to feather out the washed area otherwise, rings will be apparent when everything is dry.

■ SEATS

Seat coverings progressed from robust leatherette to even more hardwearing vinyl, before the gradual emergence of cloth in the 1970s and its dominance by the 1990s. To complicate matters,

➜ Stains and more particularly marks on a vinyl headlining (other than those that are nicotine derived) should be relatively easy to remove. However, the problem shown here stems from a leaking elevating roof and consequent tin-worm worries. Rust stains rarely disappear no matter how much elbow grease is devoted to the task.

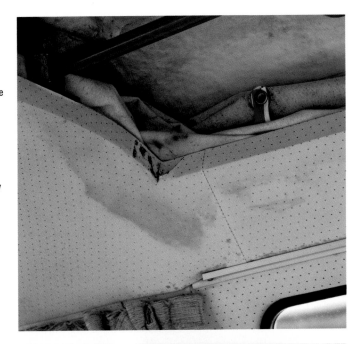

⬅ ⬆ Finding upholstery to match what Volkswagen or a Camper company provided can be near impossible. However, some fabrics have been reproduced by entrepreneurial businesses. Good luck!

Camper conversion companies originally trimmed additional seats with wonderfully patterned fabrics (think of Westfalia's plaids of the 1950s/60s) or enduring plastics. Later, when cloth had gained the ascendancy, it wasn't unheard of for a conversion company to trim the cab seats in the same material selected for the Camper's living area.

Leatherette and vinyl crack and split with age and although the latter is easy to clean, Volkswagen's preference for a basket-weave pattern doesn't make the task any easier, particularly as most seats were finished in black or other dark colours.

In some ways, cloth is even more difficult to preserve than plastic. Earlier velour offerings tended to fade easily and rot with alacrity. The more robust fabrics of later years might easily be light in colour and become grubby, while all are susceptible to the driver who insists on hanging sharp keys from his or her belt. For the perfectionist (and all concours entrants) repainting a metal panel is easy and there is no excuse for variations in shade, but finding a perfect match for perished upholstery can be a nightmare. The compromise is, of course, to re-upholster, but for the would-be purchaser considering this, the asking price for the Camper has to be taken into account. Remember also, that not every finish is easy to replicate.

■ AND FINALLY, CONCERNING INTERIORS ...

Many will be likely to be purchasing a VW Camper on the strength of its interior's appeal and the quality of the conversion. Please bear in mind that early genuine wood cabinets, panels and cupboards that haven't been polished/varnished as they should have been, will require the same kind of attention afforded to antique furniture in the home. Missing, or broken-beyond-repair items will be difficult to locate and costly to purchase. However, later laminated composite units also present problems if not in good condition. Consider the unit where a chunk of laminate has been knocked off and lost forever. How can this be repaired (and originality retained, if that is what you prefer)? Holes cut in units for long since removed ICE also present problems. Sorry to offer doom and gloom, but you must go into a purchase with your eyes wide open.

CHASSIS NUMBERS

It is always useful to know when your VW Camper was manufactured. While license plates from the mid-1960s might help to identify an original right-hand-drive vehicle in Britain and age-related plates are allocated to imports, the chassis number of the VW Camper is a much more reliable means of dating the vehicle.

FIRST-GENERATION TRANSPORTER CHASSIS NUMBERS

Between the start of production and the end of July 1955, the model year changed with the calendar year. From this point, the model year ran from 1 August to 31 July. A Transporter built in, for example, August 1960 belongs to the 1961 model year.

Until 31 December 1955 chassis numbers were up to six digits, initially prefaced by zeros to fill the gaps. These six digits were in turn prefixed by '2', '0' and a dash (-). From 1 January 1956, the '20-' was dropped and vehicles were simply numbered sequentially. With effect from 1 August 1964 (to 31 July 1969 and past the end of first-generation production, in July 1967) chassis numbers were extended to comprise nine digits in total, two model identification digits and one to represent the year, followed by six serial numbers. The examples shown here are prefaced by 23, the ones allocated to the Kombi, one of the most popular models for the Camper-conversion companies.

Date	Chassis number
December 1950	20-008 112
December 1951	20-020112
December 1952	20-041857
December 1953	20-070431
December 1954	20-110603
July 1955	20-137605
December 1955	20-160735
July 1956	191 466
July 1957	271 675
July 1958	371 275
July 1959	490 622
July 1960	632 584
July 1961	804 877
July 1962	978 018
July 1963	1 144 302
July 1964	1 328 871
1 Aug 1964	235 000 001
July 1965	235 176 339
July 1966	236 179 668
July 1967	237 148 459

The chassis number is to be found in the engine compartment of the first-generation Transporter and on an identification plate positioned on the right-hand side of the bulkhead.

SECOND-GENERATION TRANSPORTER CHASSIS NUMBERS

From 1 August 1969, and the start of the 1970 model year, to the end of second-generation Transporter production the chassis numbers were composed of ten digits. These numbers started with three identifying digits (1 = Transporter Type 2, 2 = specific model, e.g. 1 Delivery Van, 3 = model year, while the fourth, an additional digit compared to years gone by, indicated the second decade during which this kind of chassis number was used (and remains as the number two throughout). The remaining six digits formed the serial number.

Second-generation Transporters carry a metal identification plate. The chassis number is also stamped onto metal within the engine compartment (to the left 1968–71 and to the right 1972 onwards).

Date	Chassis number
1 August 1967	218 000 001
31 July 1968	218 202 251
1 August 1968	219 000 001
31 July 1969	219 238 131
1 August 1969	210 2 000 001
31 July 1970	210 2 248 837
1 August 1970	211 2 000 001
31 July 1971	211 2 276 560
1 August 1971	212 2 000 001
31 July 1972	212 2 246 946
1 August 1972	213 2 000 001
31 July 1973	213 2 254 657
1 August 1973	214 2 000 001
31 July 1974	214 2 194 943
1 August 1974	215 2 000 001
31 July 1975	215 2 155 145
1 August 1975	216 2 000 001
31 July 1976	Unknown
1 August 1976	217 2 000 001
31 July 1977	Unknown
1 August 1977	218 2 000 001
31 July 1978	Unknown
1 August 1978	219 2 000 001
31 July 1979	219 2 153 964

THIRD-, FOURTH-, AND FIFTH- GENERATION TRANSPORTER CHASSIS NUMBERS

Since 1980, standardised 17 letter and digit chassis or VIN numbers have applied to all manufacturers, making identification of the year when the VW Camper was built exceptionally easy to find. Other details are of more marginal interest ...

W	V	2	Z	Z	Z	7	0	Z	V	H	1	2	3	4	5	6
1	2	3	4	5	6	7	8	9	10	11	12	13	14	15	16	17

1,2   =   WV stands for Volkswagen's manufactured in Europe

3   =   1 (commercial vehicles - Delivery Vans and Pick-ups)

             2 (people carriers such as Caravelles, Kombis, Window Vans and Campers)

             3 (Chassis cabs)

4, 5, 6   =   filler using the letter Z, or allocated to special options or requirements

7,8   =   a two digit abbreviation of the model type, in the example 70 = T4 (24 = T3 Pick-up models, 25 = all other T3 models including Delivery Vans and Caravelle people carriers, 7H = T5)

9   =   additional filler Z

10   =   year of manufacture (see below)

11   =   Factory where manufactured. In the example H = Hanover

12–17   =   six-digit serial, which starts at 000 001 for each new model year. Volkswagen's model year ran from August to July as previously until the end of April 1999, when a change occurred. The 2000 model year started in May 1999 and concluded on 30 April 2000.

CHAPTER 7
IN WHICH YOU ARE
TOLD WHERE TO GO

This is not, and never could be, a chapter of personal recommendations. Instead, the story told contains alleged words of wisdom gained by at least part of a lifetime spent surrounded by and enthused by Volkswagens. By definition, such a statement also suggests that if your attraction to the hallowed 'V' over 'W' is purely because you believe the marque to offer more reliable service, be longer lasting, and fit for purpose for your camping aspirations rather than enthusiasm, then a good percentage of this final chapter is not for you.

SUGGESTIONS FOR THE CAMPING ENTHUSIAST
For non-VW enthusiast would-be owners, it is probably safe to assume that the aim is to purchase the newest Camper a budget will allow, to run it in stock form and enjoy it for what it is – a portable holiday home.

The advice already implied in earlier chapters would be, budget allowing, to head-off with due haste to the nearest VW Van Centre (www.volkswagenvans.co.uk) look at the VW California and the VW California Beach (yes, the Campers are at the Van Centres, not lined up with the VW cars). You will find that the second-hand examples are invariably almost new and carry a hefty price tag accordingly.

Do leave sufficient time to look at Delivery Vans, Window Vans, trim levels and anything else you can think of. Yes, you can download a brochure, or request a hard-copy version, but both are no substitute for a viewing in the metal.

Assuming you don't decide to splash out on a brand new California, or aren't tempted by the second-hand selection, your next step will be to find out what conversion companies have agents or bases in your part of the country via the web. Here you are likely to find brand new conversions, a much wider selection of second-hand models, possibly even dating back to the era of the T4 and, elsewhere, smaller companies offering bespoke conversions on vans they source for you, or you drive to them.

Alternatively, you might opt to make contact with the headquarters of one of the larger conversion companies. Some will direct you to their appointed agents, while others may well offer a list of second-hand vehicles they have on sale in addition to brand new fully converted VWs.

Assuming you still haven't found the ideal van, the next step is probably to browse the pages of a website like Autotrader. Here you will not only find private sales but also, by delving a little, established dealers offering a range of models. The only obvious downside is one of geographical distance – your ideal Camper might be 25, 50 or 250 miles from home!

Finally, there is eBay, a most useful institution and one where you will definitely find Campers of all ages on sale. Assuming your search for a T5 hasn't netted the desired result before you alight on eBay, please bear in mind that you will be buying blind unless you arrange a prior viewing (and that is enough said on the subject).

SUGGESTIONS FOR THE VW ENTHUSIAST

Let's assume first of all that you are a budding enthusiast, rather than someone already steeped in Volkswagen folklore. The guess will be that you have seen pristine first-generation models, or lovely lived-in second-generation Campers and, spurred on by a love of all things retro, you would like to be a part of a scene that clearly appears to afford a great deal of pleasure and happiness to all involved.

The first recommendation is not to rush, swept off your feet by a tornado of enthusiasm. Read about Campers (good move to buy this book) and buy, or even subscribe, to the magazines (*VW Camper and Commercial* and *VW Bus T4&5+*, both from Jazz Publishing, or *Volksworld Camper and Bus* from IPC Media). Then, try a few shows.

Such is the popularity of the VW Camper that there are a number of shows here in the UK dedicated to it, while many others are dominated by its presence. Bus Types (www.bus-types.co.uk), usually held on the outskirts of the English/Welsh border town of Oswestry in April, might be regarded as the show to kick off the main season. Camperjam (www.camperjam.com), organised by Jazz Publishing, and held at Weston Park in Shropshire each July, these days is a family highlight, while in September Busfest is marketed as 'the world's largest VW Transporter show'. Busfest (www.busfest.org) is held at the Three Counties Showground near Malvern in Worcestershire and all three shows so far mentioned are guaranteed to be teeming with all generations of VW Campers, both standard and customised.

Few VW enthusiasts with a preference for classic rather than custom Campers would omit the famous Stanford Hall show (www.stanfordhallvw.com) held on the first Sunday in May and organised by the Leicestershire and Warwickshire VW Owners Club. While T4 and beyond Campers might be thin on the ground, and the custom scene isn't catered for in concours terms, a cavalcade of well over 100 first-generation Transporters proves more than ample compensation. VW Northwest (www.vwnw.co.uk), an August event, is held in the grounds of Cheshire's Tatton Park and might be best described as a crossover event where classic and custom meet in parallel concours line-ups, something reflected in the displays and even the tastes of visitors attending.

With apologies to the organisers of all the shows omitted, attendance at two or more gatherings will hopefully have confirmed that a VW Camper is definitely for you. You will have seen VW Campers for sale in the metal (or rust) and had the opportunity to confirm the state of the market and soak up all aspects of potential ownership.

Of course, if you are uncertain whether a VW Camper is for you, you could also go down the route of hiring one from any of the numerous companies offering this service. You might even decide to take it to a VW show!

As a confirmed enthusiast by now, where are you going to buy a VW Camper or a VW Transporter to transform into a home away from home? If your choice is a T5/T6 or possibly a T4, the route described for the camping enthusiast isn't necessarily a bad one. To complete the recipe, simply add vehicles on sale at the shows, advertisers in the enthusiast magazines (both trade and private individuals).

For the first three generations, you need to spend more time scouring the magazines for companies who have made it their business to import largely rust-free Campers from sun-bleached countries such as Australia, or US States like California. Others might refurbish and sell Campers and some simply resell anything they acquire. Likewise, to become more involved in the scene and to spot a further series of vehicles for sale, it would do no harm at all to check out a few websites. Here is what many might regard as a top selection:

First generation:
The Split Screen Van Club - www.ssvc.org

Second generation:
www.forum.earlybay.com and www.thelatebay.com

Third generation:
www.club80-90.co.uk and www.brick-yard.co.uk

Through reading about Campers, talking to owners, possibly even joining one of the clubs before you own a vehicle, you will soon fall on such mysterious names as 'The Samba' and (against the rules set) Kieft and Klok. Despite www.thesamba.com being a US-based site, it is widely patronised by both UK and European residents. A wealth of VW Campers for sale can be found on the site and it will be well worth your while to keep an eye on the latest arrivals (not to mention other sections of the site). As for Kieft and Klok (www.kieftenklok.nl), it is a name that keeps cropping up and one that you wouldn't find easily without purchasing magazines, or talking to fellow enthusiasts. Of course, it is another firm that sells Campers, but rather than being down the road in the UK, K&K are based across the channel in the Netherlands; one of many that might be worth at least an ethereal visit.

↑ On holiday. Why did we wait so long?

BEHEMOTH
PUBLISHING

www.behemothpublishing.co.uk